MOORESTO
MOORESTO

Moorestown Library

3 2030 00099 1835

NJML 9.704q Vie v.11
c1981-c1984.

The Vietnam experience /

W9-ALL-177

OVERSIZED   146551

959.704q
Vie   The Vietnam experienc
             Combat photographer

v.11

Moorestown Library
Moorestown, New Jersey
08057

The Vietnam Experience

Combat Photographer

by Nick Mills
and the editors of Boston Publishing Company

Boston Publishing Company/Boston, MA

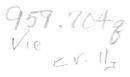

959.704g
Vie
c.v. II₂

Boston Publishing Company

President and Publisher: Robert J. George
Vice President: Richard S. Perkins, Jr.
Editor-in-Chief: Robert Manning
Managing Editor: Paul Dreyfus

Senior Writers:
   Clark Dougan, Edward Doyle, Samuel
   Lipsman, Terrence Maitland, Stephen
   Weiss
Senior Picture Editor: Julene Fischer

Staff Writer: David Fulghum
Researchers:
   Kerstin Gorham (Chief), Sandra M. Jacobs,
   Christy Virginia Keeny, Denis Kennedy,
   Carole Rulnick, Ted Steinberg, Nicole van
   Ackere

Picture Editors: Wendy Johnson, Lanng
   Tamura
Assistant Picture Editor: Kathleen A. Reidy
Picture Researchers:
   Nancy Katz Colman, Tracey Rogers, Nana
   Elisabeth Stern, Shirley L. Green
   (Washington, D.C.), Kate Lewin (Paris)
Picture Department Assistants: Suzanne M.
   Spencer, Kathryn J. Steeves

Production Editor: Patricia Leal Welch
Assistant Editor: Karen E. English
Editorial Production: Sarah E. Burns, Pamela
   George, Marta Schaefer, Amy P. Wilson

Design: Designworks, Sally Bindari

Marketing Director: Jeanne C. Gibson
Business Staff: Amy Pelletier

About the editor and author

Editor-in-chief *Robert Manning*, a long-time journalist, has previously been editor-in-chief of the *Atlantic Monthly* magazine and its press. He served as assistant secretary of state for public affairs under Presidents John F. Kennedy and Lyndon B. Johnson. He has also been a fellow at the Institute of Politics at the John F. Kennedy School of Government at Harvard University.

Author *Nick B. Mills* served in Vietnam as a combat photo team leader with the U.S. Army 221st Signal Company (Pictorial) in 1969. Now a broadcast journalist, Mr. Mills has held several positions with Boston-area radio stations and the ABC Radio Network. He received his B.S. in broadcasting and film from Boston University in 1964.

Cover photograph:

In a photograph taken by a combat photographer in the U.S. Marines, men of Company E, 2/3 Marines, battle Communist troops for Mutter's Ridge near the demilitarized zone during Operation Lancaster II in 1968.

Copyright © 1983 by Boston Publishing Company. All rights reserved. No part of this publication may be reproduced or transmitted in any form or by any means, electronic or mechanical, including photocopy, recording, or any information storage and retrieval system, without permission in writing from the publisher.

Library of Congress Catalog Card Number: 83–25870

ISBN 0-939526-08-5

10 9 8 7 6
5 4 3 2

Contents

146551

Preface

Not only was Vietnam America's longest war. It was also the most photographed. A veritable army of photographers from around the world focused their still, cinema, and TV cameras on South and North Vietnam and showered many millions of images onto the public consciousness. Uninhibited by censorship and free to venture wherever their courage or their competitiveness took them, photographers covering the South Vietnamese and American side of the war compiled a visual record that is unprecedented for its breadth and candor. Among those who compiled that record were the more than 1,500 soldiers, sailors, marines, coast guardsmen, and airmen who were assigned the front and the rear as combat photographers. This book shows the war and the people and the country of Vietnam as they captured it on film.

—The Editors

Cameras at War

Photography joined the army in the middle of the nineteenth century, while the art was still in its infancy, and it quickly became an indispensable part of military life. The union of photography and war was natural and inevitable though not always harmonious. More than words and sketches, photographs satisfied the public's intense curiosity about the state of war. They gave the chronicler and historian accurate records; they gave the soldier immutable memories. Photographs also gave the military ammunition for fighting public relations battles on the home front. Pictures of war can be instrumental in swaying public opinion, a lesson that was learned over a century ago and that backfired on the U.S. in Vietnam.

One of the first official uses of photography in war was aimed at recouping public support for Britain's war in the Crimea. Accounts in the *Times* of London of the dismal conditions at the front helped topple a government, and the new cabinet needed to quiet the dissent and rally the public behind the war effort. The young science of photography was chosen to battle the damning words of the *Times*, and in 1855 professional photographer Roger Fenton was dispatched to the Crimea with the mission of bringing back proof that the war was not going all that badly for the British. His innocuous images had the desired effect, establishing that, on one hand, people tend to trust photographs more than words and, on the other hand, that the camera can lie through its operator's choice of subject.

Since the Crimean War, photographers have followed armies and armies have used photographers, first hiring professionals such as Fenton and later recruiting and training them for the uniformed ranks. While civilian Mathew Brady was the photographic "star" of the American Civil War, the Union army and the Confederate army both employed photographers for documentary and reconnaissance purposes. Brady was essentially a free-lancer, operating under the authorization of President Lincoln to photograph the Union side of the war. Despite his place in history, Brady was not successful financially, having to rely on print sales to support his operation, which employed as many as twenty photographers at one time. Public demand for the war pictures was much lower than Brady had anticipated, both during and after the war. In 1873 Brady was in financial ruin, and his plates were auctioned off to pay overdue storage charges. The War Department bought the lot for under $3,000. Ironically, that same year the New York *Daily Graphic* became the first newspaper to use photographic illustration—a development that might have made Brady's work profitable had it come along earlier.

The photographer in uniform was an integral part of the major powers' military forces by the turn of the century and rose to primary importance in World War I. The military photographer virtually had the field to himself in the Great War, as civilian war correspondents and cameramen were barred from the fighting fronts. The photographs were tightly controlled by the military, and few were seen by the public until after the war. Even when the pictures were finally brought to light, most of the photographers remained anonymous, a condition of military photography that largely persists even today.

Technical advances in photography and an increasing awareness of its importance led to the incredibly voluminous photodocumentation of the second world war by both the Allied and Axis forces. The U.S. military photo effort started slowly but steadily increased until photo teams were attached to all combat units of the army, navy, and air force. These military photographers covered every phase and front of the war, sending back to Washington such quantities of pictures that to this day the material has reportedly not all been seen and catalogued. To the U.S. effort, add the photographic output of the British, French, German, Russian, and Japanese militaries, and the total soars to uncounted millions of images. Although the military photographers had much greater access to the fighting and took far more pictures than civilian press photographers, most of their material remained under wraps until after the war, and when the pictures were released the photographers themselves remained anonymous.

By the end of World War II, war photography was approaching its centennial. The technical advances of that century made possible the quantity and quality of

Roger Fenton's photographic darkroom van used during the Crimean War, 1854.

the coverage of World War II, the kind of coverage of which the early war photographers could not have even dreamed. The earliest cameras, while bulky and cumbersome by themselves, were virtually useless unless accompanied by a horse-drawn darkroom. It was not until the end of the nineteenth century that the wet collodion process gave way to dry plates and celluloid-backed film. These developments, coupled with the introduction of smaller cameras, gave the photographer much more mobility. The speed of the films also increased, allowing faster shutter speeds, which in turn made possible the first true action photographs. When Brady photographed the Civil

Mathew Brady's photographic outfit near Petersburg, Va., during the Civil War.

War, his subjects had to be posed—or dead. The first action shots were taken at about the turn of the century, during the Spanish-American and Boer wars.

Almost simultaneously, American newspapers were able to improve the half-tone process to the point that photographs became staple fare in the daily newspaper. These two technological advances were the essential handmaidens of the lasting marriage of photography and journalism.

The marriage wasn't truly consummated, though, until 1925, the year Leica's 35MM range finder camera went on the market. Although slow to gain wide acceptance in military photography, the 35MM camera was readily embraced by men who would set the standards for the new breed of photojournalists, men

such as Robert Capa, David Seymour, Lucien Aigner, and Alfred Eisenstadt. Where the earliest war photographers had to cope with cameras the size of cupboards plus their mother-ship darkrooms, the new breed could tuck a couple of cameras into jacket pockets and photograph virtually anything they saw. War photography at once became more intimate; photographers could get closer to the action and closer to their subjects—and closer to danger. This, of course, created a new demand: action photos.

While military photographers could simply be ordered into the action and were constantly exposed to the dangers, some of the civilian war photographers and correspondents found ways to minimize the hazards while feeding their editors steady diets of action pictures. In-

deed, there have been accusations (by Philip Knightley in his book *The First Casualty* and by O. D. Gallagher, war correspondent for the London *Daily Express*) that even the most sacred icon of war photography, Robert Capa's *Death of a Loyalist Soldier*, was faked, although there is no positive proof. The picture was taken during the Spanish Civil War in 1936. In earlier times pictures were commonly staged for practical reasons, to accommodate the technical limitations of the camera. By the 1930s, when true action photography was possible, the demands of editors, the restricted access to war zones, and the trepidations of the cameramen led to the staging of some pictures. In Vietnam there were instances of civilian correspondents buying pictures from combat photographers, and it was not uncommon for a correspondent to hire Vietnamese photographers for combat assignments. Also, television reporters were known to hire GI "actors" to stage action backgrounds for their reports. One famous network television correspondent faked an action background right in the middle of the huge Long Binh post, possibly the most sophisticated and secure U.S. base in Vietnam, in a wooded area called "Monkey Jungle."

Not that the military photographers were immune to this affliction: the image-conscious brass would occasionally order both still pictures and motion picture footage tailor-made for public relations purposes or training films. Also, some individual photographers must surely have faked some action shots either to impress their superiors, to sell to civilian correspondents, or to provide war souvenirs for their buddies.

How much of this type of material found its way into the official file is unknown. But we have every confidence that the combat pictures presented in this book are genuine. Many of the individual photographers have been located and have given detailed accounts of the circumstances in which their pictures were taken.

The Vietnam War was a new experience for photojournalists, because for the first time they were allowed to operate in complete freedom. They were not censored and were encouraged to photograph and report on the conflict and were transported by the military to wherever they wanted to go. It was a different kind of war for America. In the beginning the U.S. did not play a combat role and made a great effort to justify its presence there by emphasizing the "good guy" aspect of the mission. The U.S. wanted the Vietnam story told and invited correspondents to help tell it. Later, the open-eye policy would backfire as the more sordid aspects of the war made their way out to TV screens, front pages, and magazine covers. By then it was too late for censorship. Some correspondents who fell from grace with the U.S. military leaders were barred from Vietnam, but widespread restrictions would only have further inflamed the antiwar movement.

While making coverage of the war easy for civilian correspondents, the U.S. military also assigned hundreds of photographers in uniform to tours in Vietnam to cover the war from within. These men often worked in the same manner as their civilian counterparts and under a broad mandate to fully document the activities of the U.S. military in Southeast Asia. They photographed all branches of the military in all aspects of their lives in Vietnam, and they did so in a way the civilians could not: as insiders, brothers, members of the family. They wore the same uniforms, ate the same food, slept in the same tents, and drew the same pay as the men they were photographing. They also took the same risks and suffered the same casualties. They worked virtually unrestricted in the field, many of them in places and combat situations civilian photographers did not reach. Together, over the years, the combat photographers compiled a large body of work, a valuable record of the way it was in Vietnam.

The first military photographers sent to Vietnam were dispatched from the Army Pictorial Center in New York City, where the peacetime army produced documentaries and training films. Enlisted photographers Specialist 5 James Twitty and Sergeant Lucius Croft were assigned in March 1962 to make a quick trip to Vietnam to photograph the activities of the U.S. military advisers who were training the South Vietnamese for their war against the Communist guerrillas, the Vietcong. Twitty and Croft never made it: Their plane vanished without a trace in the Pacific. Another photo team was formed at the APC and made a brief trip to Vietnam, but, as Lieutenant Colonel (ret.) Claude Bache recalls, they only spent a couple of weeks and didn't accomplish much. Then, Bache says, "the word came down from the Pentagon that we were forming DASPO," the Department of the Army Special Photo Office.

DASPO was born in the spring of 1962 with its headquarters at the APC, and three detachments were formed to give worldwide coverage of army activities. The Pacific detachment set up housekeeping in Saigon and rotated personnel from Honolulu into Vietnam for three-month, or longer, periods. Until the American build-up, when the other branches of the service arrived in force, military photo coverage of the Vietnam War was largely DASPO's responsibility.

When the U.S. sent combat troops to Vietnam in 1965, other photographers arrived with them and DASPO's coverage was augmented by combat photographers from the army, navy, air force, Marine Corps, and the Coast Guard. Brigade-sized units had photographers assigned to their information offices, and these men would go out in the field with the battalions, companies, platoons, or patrols, photographing their activities. Later still, the army formed a purely photographic unit—the 221st Signal Company, which absorbed the photo components of the 69th Signal Battalion and the 593d Signal Battalion. The 221st served as the manpower company for the Southeast Asia Pictorial Center (SEAPC), which was set up like an in-country DASPO. SEAPC had motion picture and still photo capability, its own lab complex for still photo processing and printing, and six permanent detachments from the DMZ to the delta.

In peacetime the navy routinely assigns photographers, called photographer's mates, to cover all navy activities and ceremonies. Early navy advisory duties in Vietnam were photographed by these men. The navy also employed an elite photo operation, the Pacific Fleet Combat Camera Group, which rotated motion picture and still photographers into Vietnam for 120-day tours twice a year. Combat Camera Group-Pacific (CCGPAC) had a detachment in Saigon and lab facilities there and in Cam Ranh Bay and Da Nang. The group had about twenty photographers in Vietnam at all times during the years of the U.S. combat role there, and of those twenty, three or four were still photographers. Some of

these photo mates had learned their craft at the elbow of a veteran in a navy lab, but many were formally trained as photographers and journalists in the navy schools in Pensacola, Florida. The navy also offered advanced courses in photojournalism and cinematography at Syracuse University, Rochester Institute of Technology, and the University of Southern California.

The Marine Corps had no photo school of its own, so marine photographers were trained at either navy or army schools. Journalism training took place at the Defense Information School at Fort Benjamin Harrison, Indiana, and the marine combat correspondent was usually skilled in both photography and journalism. In Vietnam, still photographers worked out of a division or wing information office, or out of the Combat Information Bureau in Da Nang on assignments with *Leatherneck* magazine. Early in the Vietnam War the marine combat correspondents trained for Vietnam by going through the combat orientation course at Camp Pendleton, California. Later, it was decided the additional training was needed, so the corps established an eight-week Combat Correspondent Orientation Course at Camp Pendleton to teach the correspondents how to best operate in a combat situation, both as journalists and photographers. Following the eight-week course, they went through the regular infantry orientation course before heading for Vietnam.

Some of the best Marine Corps combat photography was done by the *Leatherneck* staff, which operated out of Tokyo. Teams of photographers were sent into Vietnam on six-month rotations. In-country, these men functioned on their own, just as civilian correspondents do, following the action and shipping their material to the magazine.

Air force photographers were trained at Lowry Air Force Base in Denver in a six-month course, which trained them in picture-taking and lab techniques. At Lowry there was also a short course for combat photographers, in which the photographers accompanied army units on maneuvers. For those who were headed

Specialist 4 Eugene Campbell, a combat photographer of the 221st Signal Company, in the field with ARVN troops near Can Tho in 1969.

for aerial combat photography, there was flight school, to acclimate the photographer to high-performance aircraft, and jungle survival school in the Philippines—in case they got shot down. In Vietnam, air force photographers were clustered at the major air bases such as Tan Son Nhut, Bien Hoa, and Phu Cat. They were organized into such units as the 600th Photo Squadron or the 460th Recon Tech Wing. A small, select group of air force photographers, both still and motion picture, was assigned to the 352d Combat Documentary unit at Travis Air Force Base in California. These photographers functioned largely as free-lancers in Vietnam, with carte blanche to document any and all air force activities in Southeast Asia.

Although the military photographer had the advantage of being an "insider," in one way the uniform was a drawback. Technically, all the pictures shot by military photographers belonged to the military. While the photographer was virtually unrestricted in what he could photograph, many of his pictures were later lost in the bureaucratic editing process. For example, the work of an army photographer would be sent, with captions, to an office in the Pentagon for review by a mostly civilian staff. Some pictures would be selected for the permanent collection, some might be kept but classified, and the rest would be destroyed. Since pictures selected for the permanent file would be available to the public, the staff was sensitive to pictures that might put the army in a less-than-flattering light. The reason for destroying a picture might be as flimsy as its showing a soldier without a hat or shirt or with a cigarette hanging from his lips.

To their credit, the staffs of the various still photo depositories retained a large body of valuable Vietnam photography. They did so while coping with a flood of material—10,000 pictures a month from the army alone during the peak of U.S. involvement, according to one former staff member. Also, many photographers managed to retain prints, duplicate transparencies, and even some negatives of images that might otherwise have been lost forever. Thanks to their preservationist instincts in addition to the work of the official archivists, a substantial body of the work done in Vietnam by the combat photographers is still available.

Some military photographers didn't have to contend with this editing process back in Washington. They worked for the various military publications, such as *Stars & Stripes* and *Leatherneck,* and they functioned almost exactly like civilian photojournalists, flying to battle scenes anywhere in Vietnam, shooting their pictures, and rushing them out to meet publishing deadlines. In fact, *Stars & Stripes* functioned so much like a civilian newspaper that one U.S. colonel nicknamed it "the Hanoi Herald" and branded as "treason" a story by one of its combat correspondents, Bob Hodierne. (Some of Hodierne's work is included in this book.)

The classic example of the military photographers' freedom in the field is army sergeant Ronald Haeberle's photographs of the My Lai massacre. The pictures would probably never have seen the light of day if Haeberle had turned them all in to his command, but he turned in just his black and white film and pocketed a roll of color slides, which were eventually published. Haeberle thus became the best-known combat photographer of the Vietnam War, for photographing America's most inglorious and shameful hour of the conflict.

The Vietnam experience was one of such intensity that it remains with Vietnam veterans in surpassing clarity. Not only can the veteran recall events, but also he can still hear the guns, smell the smoke, and feel the heat, dust, and fear. He can also recall the camaraderie, the good times, and the intimate bond with his buddies—and the sharp grief brought by their deaths. These photographs will no doubt bring many vivid memories to the surface.

This collection of photographs also tries to present a well-rounded picture of the Vietnam experience; not just the mud and the blood but the country and its people and slices of everyday life with its wide variety of conditions, occupations, and relationships. In addition, several of the photographers who took the pictures used here have related their experiences for the book. Their words add an extra dimension to the pictures, deepening our understanding of, and our involvement with, the photographs.

In the Field

Charlie Company, 1st Battalion, 3d Marines, 3d Division, moves out through morning mist in the Cam Lo Valley sixty kilometers south of the demilitarized zone on a search and destroy mission, August 24, 1969.

Going out into the field in Vietnam could mean a number of things, none of them easy or pleasant. "The Field" was where the war was, where Charlie was, and the soldier went out there to find him and fight him. Depending on what kind of outfit the soldier fought in, the way to go into the field might be in the air, on boats, in wheeled or tracked vehicles, or on his own two feet. Going on foot was "humping the boonies," hauling a heavy combat load through rice fields, across rivers, up hills and mountains, through jungles and elephant grass, in mud, sand, or dust, under a cruel sun or in a monsoon rain.

Sometimes it was a walk in the sun, a Sunday drive, but no one called it that until the unit was back at the base camp because at any point any number of bad things could happen. At every step were the myriad dangers of Vietnam—ambush, booby trap, land mine, sniper.

Many combat soldiers were sent into the field on their first day in Vietnam and rarely left it until they went home. They spent virtually their entire tour humping the boonies or setting up night ambushes and could count on their fingers the number of nights they slept on something as luxurious as a folding cot.

The army calls him "The Ultimate Weapon"—the infantryman. Throughout history the foot soldier has been the basic unit of warfare, the one who performs the elemental dirty work of war. Over the ages the uniforms and the weapons have changed, but the job of the foot soldier has changed hardly at all. He's still the one who has to muck it out with the enemy at close range, the one who ultimately conquers and holds—or loses—the real estate. In Vietnam the foot soldier picked up a new nickname: the "grunt."

Whether in the field with a squad or a platoon or even a battalion, the combat soldier could feel very much alone in the thick jungles and tall grasses. One of the loneliest and spookiest jobs in the world was walking point in Vietnam.

Opposite. A navy SEAL on a search and destroy operation in the Mekong Delta, September 1967.

Left. A 1st Infantry Division NCO during Operation Billings near Long Binh in June 1967.

Wherever a soldier went in Vietnam he could be sure of one thing: It wouldn't be easy. The going could get very wet, very muddy, or just plain tricky.

Opposite above. In July 1966, near Dak To, paratroopers of the 101st Airborne Division cross a rope and bamboo bridge during Operation Beauregard.

Opposite below. A wet pursuit of the Vietcong.

Left. Mekong Delta mud slows down a SEAL team member as he makes his way ashore from a navy boat in May 1970.

Above. A MACV adviser on patrol with South Vietnamese troops in the Mekong Delta near Can Tho, 1968.

In the early days of the war, the U.S. limited its presence in Vietnam to advisers. These highly trained men worked in the field alone or in small teams, trying to mold the Vietnamese soldiers and civilians into a respectable fighting force. As they trained the Vietnamese these advisers also learned about a kind of war Americans were unfamiliar with and about an enemy who fought with booby traps and poisoned stakes and hid in tunnels.

Opposite. U.S. Army adviser Captain Ernest Cherry, Jr.,and Captain Than Thanh Sang of the 48th ARVN Infantry Regiment survey the countryside as their helicopter heads for an LZ.

Above. On January 28, 1963, American Special Forces advisers and the montagnards they are training move out on a mission in Ba To.

Left. A U.S. Marine adviser listens in on the briefing of ARVN troops before a mission on February 20, 1963.

Above. Navy SEALs cruise through the Mekong Delta in October 1968.

Right. A tunnel rat goes into action, 1969.

Opposite above. Sergeant J.M. Jones of Company F, 2d Battalion, 7th Marines, and his scout dog stay low as the company opens fire on a Communist position in May 1970.

Opposite below. A tunnel rat of the 25th Infantry Division crawls through a Vietcong tunnel complex near Cu Chi on August 4, 1966.

The tunnels created a new job for the U.S. troops: that of "tunnel rat." The rats had to be fairly small men, as were the Vietnamese who dug the tunnels. They also needed the guts to descend alone with flashlight and pistol (a rifle was too awkward in the tunnels) into the dark, twisting passageways to find the enemy. An encounter with the Vietcong could be deadly. The firing of a weapon or the blast of a grenade in a tunnel could cause concussion and deafness—and those were but the minor consequences of tunnel combat.

Another specialized soldier was the scout dog handler. The dogs could hear and smell things that humans could not. They were credited with saving many lives by sniffing out enemy soldiers, tunnels, booby traps, and supply caches. The scout dogs and their handlers shared close relationships.

There were a number of small, specialized units in Vietnam that operated in shadowy and secretive ways, such as Navy SEAL (Sea, Air, and Land) teams; long range patrols, which would spend a week or more in the field observing enemy movements; and snipers who fought the war one well-placed shot at a time, in marked contrast to the frenzied firing of a rifleman in a firefight.

Preceding pages. Men of the 1st Infantry Division aboard their armored personnel carriers secure a section of road in the Michelin rubber plantation near An Loc, northwest of Saigon.

Left. APCs of the 199th Infantry Brigade head for base camp after a sweep south of Saigon on April 9, 1968.

Above. During Operation Daring Rebel in May 1969, tanks of the 1st Battalion, 26th Marines, come under sniper fire on Barrier Island, southeast of Da Nang.

Going into the field on wheels or tracks was generally safer and a lot less tiring than going on foot. Armored personnel carriers (APCs) and tanks gave the grunt a lot more protection and firepower, although even the tanks were vulnerable to mines and antitank weapons. And when a tank broke down in the field the rule of thumb was to move a safe distance away from it, since enemy mortarmen were quick to zero in on such a prize.

An army captain who had been commanding a tank squadron in the Kontum area related this story: He said his tankers were supporting an infantry unit on a sweep one day when they got into a firefight with some North Vietnamese regulars who had just come down the Ho Chi Minh Trail into South Vietnam. This was their first combat action and, after firing at the tanks with their AK47 rifles to no effect, some of the NVA surrendered. Upon close inspection of the American tanks they became furious, and one of them kicked the big tread of a tank in anger and disgust. They explained to the Americans through an ARVN interpreter that in Hanoi they had been told the American tanks were made of plywood and could be easily defeated.

One of the principal hazards of riding to work in Vietnam was the abundance of enemy land mines. Sweeping the roads with mine detectors was time consuming but necessary.

Opposite. 5th Infantry Division troops aboard an M48 tank.

Above. A truckload of marines of the 1st Battalion, 26th Marines, on the move during Operation Daring Rebel.

Left. In July 1970, elements of the 3d Squadron, 5th Cavalry, 9th Infantry Division, refuel after a day of patrolling near the Laotian border.

Above and right. Paratroopers of the 101st Airborne Division carry out a practice jump over Kontum Province in 1967.

Opposite. A navy river patrol boat makes a fast run down one of the many rivers of the Mekong Delta.

Parachuting into combat became a rarity during the Vietnam War; instead of jumping from a plane, airborne troops were carried to the battlefield by helicopter. But U.S. paratroopers did make several practice jumps in Vietnam and the 503d Airborne Brigade conducted a combat parachute assault during Operation Junction City, a search and destroy mission in February 1967.

Boats and ships were important in Vietnam as the country had a long coast-line, a number of major rivers, and vast swamplands. The army, navy, marines, and Coast Guard all used a variety of craft, from little shallow-draft airboats to aircraft carriers, to control the waterways and add firepower to land-based operations. The river patrol boats were fast and nimble, capable of turning completely around at full speed in their own length (about thirty feet). They were not heavily armored, though, which made them vulnerable to riverbank ambushes as they patrolled the narrow waterways.

Navy patrol craft loaded with Vietnamese marines patrol a narrow channel on the Ca Mau Peninsula in April 1969.

Above. A monitor boat—called a "Zippo" because of its flame-throwing capability—from River Assault Flotilla 1 of the Mobile Riverine Force burns out potential enemy ambush sites along a stream bank in the Mekong Delta, July 12, 1968.

Left. Crewmen aboard a strike assault boat (STAB) on high-speed patrol near the Cambodian border on June 20, 1970.

First Blood

by Marv Wolf

I was in the third chopper in a daisy chain of five, each about thirty seconds behind the other. I sat on my flak jacket, surrounded by cameras and my M16, in the left-hand door-gunner's seat. I had a vague hope that a slug coming up through the soft aluminum belly of the chopper wouldn't make me a eunuch. The door-gunner was back at An Khe, safe. I was in his seat because a Huey can haul only so many guys—there were seven other grunts aboard—and I wanted pictures of this assault landing by a company of the 1st Battalion, 5th Cavalry. I'd been in the country a couple of months since arriving in August 1965, but this was my first air assault.

The first chopper dipped into the clearing that was to be our LZ and I heard the pilot say something quick and terse in the headphones I was wearing, but I couldn't make it out. In seconds he lifted out again, empty, and the next chopper disappeared into a hole in the green jungle. As we slowed to make our descent a huge fireball erupted just ahead of us. Our pilot cursed and pulled pitch.

We flew through the top of the fireball.

Marv Wolf, third from left, at Bong Son, 1966.

I was conscious mostly of the smell of burned hair and the sudden drying out of my damp clothes. Then we were jinking left and right at low altitude as we struggled clear of the area.

What follows took under a minute to happen but seemed like an entire lifetime. We went around in a big circle, with the other loaded choppers, and the pilots yelled back and forth in my earphones. The gist of it was that there were eight grunts down there from the first lift in and an unknown number from the second. The pilots were deciding, then and there, how best to get back into the LZ so our grunts could save the guys already inserted.

My gut told me that the risk of staying on the chopper was less because it was all going to be over in a few seconds. If I stayed on the ground I'd be both closer to danger and exposed to it longer. I really didn't want to get off that helicopter. And I didn't really see what difference it would make to the war, to my country, to my outfit.

But I also knew that I had volunteered to come to Vietnam as a photographer, that I had volunteered to go with this outfit, and that if I did get some pictures they might be seen by people all over the world. Maybe this wasn't important in the grand scheme of things, but it was important to me. It was the job I'd been given to do.

I leapt out with the rest from three or four feet up and hit the ground running, feeling vaguely ridiculous with an M16 in

my left hand and an ancient Speed Graphic in my right. The ten yards to the comparative cover of the tree line felt like an entire football field. The camera bag banging on my left hip seemed to weigh a ton. I don't know why I wasn't shot, because I was the last to reach cover by a country mile.

I heard the chopper rev up behind me and hover out amid a flurry of shots, but I couldn't find the strength to turn around for a look. In a few seconds the volume of small arms fire around me rose to a ragged crescendo and I heard the next chopper hover in. I snaked around ninety degrees, then rose up on one elbow. The guys running toward me while the chopper lumbered skyward made a great composition and I held up the Graphic, then snapped the shutter.

One of the newcomers threw himself down near me, and as I recocked the shutter I realized that I hadn't removed the dark slide—I hadn't made an exposure. This wasn't exactly the first time I'd used that camera, and it wasn't the first time I'd made that mistake. But this time it seemed hilarious, and I started to laugh at myself.

I took the dark slide out, shoved it in a pocket, and raised up again, looking for something, anything, to photograph. Another chopper landed behind us and the guy who'd just arrived started shooting into the woods, at what I'll never know. I thought that was funny, too, and so I laughed again. He glanced at me with pain in his eyes—and then he started to laugh too. He pointed at the Graphic. The whole front of the camera was bashed in, probably from a ricochet, and here I was trying to take his picture. "Hey, PIO," he called, "this mean I ain't gonna get my picture in *Stars & Stripes*?"

That's when I knew everything was going to be okay for me. I got out my other camera, my treasured Leica IIIC, and started doing my job.

Marv Wolf served in Vietnam with the 1st Air Cavalry from July 1965 to November 1966. He arrived in Vietnam a private first class and left a second lieutenant after a direct appointment to the officer ranks. Today he lives in southern California and works as a free-lance writer and photo-journalist.

Men of the 1st Squadron, 9th Cavalry, 1st Cavalry Division (Airmobile), leap from a chopper near Chu Lai during Operation Oregon in 1967.

To say there were a lot of helicopters in Vietnam is like saying there are a lot of yellow taxis in New York City—it simply understates the case. Helicopters seemed to be everywhere and do everything in Vietnam. The helicopter was workhorse and war-horse. It took men into combat and brought them out again. It provided firepower; it brought supplies and food. The helicopter carried the wounded to hospitals, brought out the dead, rescued the living. In the final hours when the last Americans fled Saigon, it was the helicopter that lifted them out to the waiting ships offshore; the last U.S. soldiers to leave Vietnam left aboard a helicopter. Beats there a Vietnam veteran's heart that does not quicken at the sound of a helicopter? Fat, whapping angels of mercy and vengeance! They were also fascinating to photographers, always managing to look somehow out of place in the sky, metal bugs defying aerodynamics.

Retaking an LZ. Above. A CH-46 lifts off with combat-ready marines headed for LZ Catapult, an abandoned LZ just south of the DMZ being reactivated by the marines. Photographer Landon Thorne captioned this picture, "Worshipers of Chopper Cult climb to the altar to ascend into Heaven in Chopper God's belly."

Right. The enemy, who had occupied the abandoned LZ, was still around when the marines landed. The first two CH-46s to set down were disabled by command-deto-nated mines.

Above. The other pilots headed for this out-cropping just below the LZ and, fearing more mines, "tailgated" without actually setting down while the marines unloaded.

Left. The marines greet the dawn on LZ Catapult with a campfire for warmth and hot coffee. The mountains in January were chilly and damp, and a fire felt good after a long night's watch.

Right. A howitzer and its ammo arrive at Firebase Musket.

Opposite above. The battery is up and firing.

Opposite below. The fire mission over, the artillerymen wait for their ride home to Phu Bai.

36

The term "airmobile" didn't apply just to infantry soldiers. The artillery was also airmobile and the big guns could be quickly brought within range of the action. Here, an artillery battery of the 101st Airborne Division is en route from its base at Phu Bai to Fire Support Base Musket, fifty kilometers away. The entire battery was up and ready for its fire mission within thirty minutes of its departure from Phu Bai. After pounding away all day with its 105MM howitzers, shelling 130 targets, the men wait in the late afternoon mist for their lift back to base camp.

Above. On April 29, 1970, just before the U.S. incursion into Cambodia, men of the 25th Infantry Division fly by helicopter toward the border. Shortly after the troops landed, U.S. artillery rounds hit the LZ, by mistake killing several soldiers.

Opposite. A marine of the 3d Marine Division during Operation Lancaster, southwest of Con Thien, November 6, 1967.

For the infantry, "commuting" to work by helicopter was a mixed blessing. Getting there was *all* the fun. The ride was cool and refreshing and the view was terrific. The problem was that one had to land, and that could be dangerous. Everyone's heart was in his throat as the chopper descended to the LZ; everyone hoped it wouldn't be "hot." Once the soldiers were on the ground the helicopters left. After the day's work the "taxis" were called to come take the men home. They were a welcome sight, and the ride back to base was rich with feelings of relief and weariness and the anticipation of showers and beer, hot food and sleep.

Above. Helicopters of the 187th Assault Helicopter Company, "The Crusaders," head back to their base at Tay Ninh with troops of the 25th Infantry Division after a day of fighting inside Cambodia in May 1970.

When in the field, a man needed to know where he was and to let others know where he was. If he wandered into the wrong grid square he might bring his own artillery down on his head. Brigadier General Thomas "Long Tom" Rienzi had a plaque on his office wall that said, "When you're out of commo [communications] you're out of beer." The military in Vietnam was equipped with a sophisticated array of communication equipment ranging from massive tropo–scatter dishes to backpack radios. An infantry company in the field carried with it a little forest of antennas, vital links to headquarters, artillery, and air support. In the field it was essential to keep in touch and know where you were if you were to get home safely.

Left. A Canadian who came to the U.S. to join the marines and volunteer for Vietnam duty serves as a radioman with the 26th Marines during Operation Meade River near Da Nang in the "Dodge City" area of Highway 1 in November 1968.

Above. A platoon leader with the 9th Infantry Division stays low as he communicates with other units during a search of a Vietcong hideout near Dong Tam in July 1969.

Right. Where are we? The radio-telephone operator and team leader of a 9th Infantry Division unit try to find out, July 1969.

Opposite. Sergeant Juan S.N. Cruz of the 2d Battalion, 12th Cavalry, 1st Air Cav, leads a long-range patrol back to camp near Bong Son in December 1965.

One Day at a Time

Men of the 2d Battalion, 26th Marines, occupy a bomb-crater bivouac in "No Man's Land," east of Da Nang in February 1969.

The Vietnam experience was rich in variety and colored by a wide spectrum of conditions and events. The common denominator was The War; it was the only reason anyone was there, and of course it permeated everyone's life wherever he was and whatever his job. Within the context of the war and the particular confines of a soldier's mission, life went on. The Americans ate, drank, slept, worked, played, worshiped, and made love. Some went to the beach on Sunday; most went on "vacations." But the fact of the war altered each of these common-place activities, transforming necessities into luxuries and luxuries into fantasies, at least for some servicemen. For many support troops, life was more nearly "normal"—meals in a dining hall, sleep in a room with a real bed. But for others, especially the combat soldiers, a muddy shell crater might serve as both mess hall and barracks. Some Americans were able to live with their girlfriends; for others the endless daydream of perfect nights with exotic women became, in reality, brief, boozy encounters with whores in the "boom-boom rooms."

For most of the Americans, Vietnam was the most intense experience of their lives, far different from anything they had ever done or would ever do again. And most, whether the sum total of it was good, bad, or even awful, would not choose to give up their memory of it.

Opposite. A member of the 1/26 Marines lunches on C-rations in an abandoned village on Barrier Island southeast of Da Nang, May 1969.

Left. LZ Charlie Brown, near Duc Pho along the central coast, 1969.

Above. Private First Class Larry Joyner of the 196th Light Infantry Brigade, Americal Division, writes home in mid-1969.

Opposite. Thinking of home: a soldier of the 5th Infantry Division (Mechanized).

Mail from home, word from The World: One of the most precious commodities in Vietnam or any other war zone.

Writing back wasn't always easy, and sometimes a lot had to be left out so the folks back home wouldn't worry too much.

Free time in Vietnam was often spent just thinking and thoughts were usually of home.

The most common ailment in Vietnam was homesickness. No one really wanted to be there, but everyone made the best of it, observing holidays, birthdays, anniversaries, and other special occasions even in difficult circumstances.

Above. Specialist 4 George McCormick of the 9th Infantry Division posts a reminder that home is halfway around the world.

Right. A C-ration pound cake and waterproof matches help a soldier mark his birthday in the boonies in 1970.

The water in your canteen was usually warm and tasted of the plastic canteen, but you couldn't get enough of it. Here, soldiers of the 25th Infantry Division take a break from their patrol near Duc Pho on August 31, 1967.

A rule to live by in the military, especially in a war zone: never stand when you can sit, never sit when you can lie down, never stay awake if you can sleep—because you never know when your next chance will come.

Keeping clean was a challenge met in creative ways, and war or not, a trooper had to shave.

Opposite above. An 82d Airborne Division trooper makes the most of a break, August 3, 1969.

Opposite below. A latrine at Firebase Bandit II.

Above. An artilleryman shaves after a long night of guard duty at a 1st Air Cav firebase in the central highlands, 1966.

Left. Specialist 4 Reginald Moore of the 196th Infantry Brigade, American Division, washes his hair in his steel pot.

Left. Members of the 9th Marines, 3d Marine Division, huddle under ponchos on September 27, 1968, during a break from their operation in the DMZ.

Above. Three marines cool off in a stream near Da Nang on February 18, 1970.

The weather in Vietnam was either wet or hot, and when it was wet you couldn't stay dry enough. When it was hot you couldn't stay wet enough.

Above. Marines attend Catholic services during Operation Meade River along Highway 1 near Da Nang, November 1968.

Right. A chaplain holds services in Pleiku for four combat photographers of the 221st Signal Company who were killed when their helicopter was shot down in Cambodia in May 1970.

Opposite. Chaplain (Captain) Peter Kraak and Chaplain (Captain) John DeSaegher of the 25th Infantry Division conduct a baptism at Cu Chi on July 17, 1966.

Ammo-box altars and camouflaged vestments—these were the hallmarks of field services in Vietnam. The chaplains went where the troops were, to minister to their spiritual needs and often to administer last rites or conduct services for the dead. These field services were among the most poignant scenes of the war, for here were young men brought suddenly face to face with eternity, straining to hear the voice of God above the din of armies. Some men clung to the organized religions they had been brought up with. Others put their faith in charms, amulets, and totems. One marine credits his survival to an unwashed T-shirt, which he keeps to this day in a plastic bag in a bureau drawer, afraid if he washes it he will die.

Above, clockwise from upper left: A tiger shot on patrol by a unit of the 5th Infantry Division (Mechanized); Wrapped up in the Cam Ranh Bay motor pool mascot; "Charlie," mascot of the 501st Signal Battalion; and a homing pigeon used by recon units of the 101st Airborne.

Opposite. Feeding the geese-guardians of Saigon's "Y" Bridge.

Poor was the unit that didn't have a mascot or pet in this animal-rich land. Dogs were common but some units went in for more exotic pets.

Tigers, however, could become casualties of the war. Every so often one of these magnificent cats would be shot and killed by patrolling GIs.

Only a fraction of the troops who served in Vietnam were combat soldiers. The rest were support personnel who built the bases, drove the trucks, serviced the aircraft, cooked the food, sorted the mail, did the paperwork, and performed all the myriad tasks that kept the military machine running. But in some measure they all shared in the Vietnam experience: They were all exposed to the war.

One of the more unusual jobs in Vietnam was that of keeper of the geese. Someone—obviously a farm boy—had come up with the idea of using geese as watch birds to sound the alarm at the approach of any stranger. Geese are not only very loud birds, they have a well-developed territorial imperative and resent any intrusion on their turf. Flocks of geese such as these were used successfully to guard bridges and checkpoints.

Just as the basic foot soldier was essential in combat, the basic manual laborer was essential to building the roads, bases, and airports the Americans constructed in Vietnam.

A navy Seabee works on a road near the DMZ.

War? What war? The U.S. command brought in boatloads of toys for the men to play with, everything from go-carts to violins. There was surfing, sailing, miniature golf. Just about everyone got a chance to spend a day or so at a beach where he could pretend he wasn't in Vietnam. Large bases featured Olympic-size swimming pools and air-conditioned libraries, softball fields, and basketball courts. Even the meanest base would have a net and a volleyball.

Above. Lance Corporal Pat Kelly of the Company G, 2/7 Marines, 1st Marine Division, and his brother Hospitalman 3d Class Mike Kelly, 3d Medical Battalion, enjoy the surf at Chu Lai on June 27, 1966, during a two-day reunion.

Left. A competitor races in the Da Nang 500 Racing classic on May 30, 1966.

A soldier could requisition from Special Services enough musical instruments to form a band or maybe the army band would entertain.

If he were too far out in the boonies, with a little ingenuity and a few raw materials a man could rig up a washtub bass and make his own music.

Above. Private Andrew Hahto and Private David Peterson play in the 226th Army Band at Tan Son Nhut air base.

Right. A GI plunks on a makeshift string bass in the central highlands.

Opposite. An air force NCO sits on his doorstep on Soul Alley near Tan Son Nhut air base.

In the earlier days of the war, U.S. military personnel on leave in Saigon could put on civilian clothes and play tourist. Even after the 1968 Tet attacks it was possible to enjoy sightseeing, shopping, and carousing in Saigon, but the city was a much more tense place.

In the early days it was also fairly common for American servicemen to live in civilian housing, often with a Vietnam-ese girlfriend. After the Tet offensive this was largely prohibited, but some servicemen managed to continue the arrangement with the tacit approval of their superiors. Near the big Tan Son Nhut air base there was a street known as "Soul Alley" where a number of black soldiers lived with Vietnamese women and commuted to their jobs on the base.

One of the major American imports to Vietnam was the visiting celebrity. The stars would be fitted with jungle fatigues, briefed by the brass, and flown all around the country to visit firebases and hospitals where they would shake hands, sign autographs, and pose for pictures—all in the interest of boosting morale. Often a military photographer would be assigned to cover the celebrity's visit, and the star would get to keep the pictures for stateside promotional purposes.

The star of stars was Bob Hope, and his show was the act of acts. Amphitheaters were built at major bases for the Bob Hope Show and Hope was guaranteed a full house. Most GIs wanted to see the show, of course, but to erase any doubt about the seats being filled units were required to send given quotas of men to the show. For a grunt in the field, getting a day off to be flown out of the bush for the Bob Hope Show was a big treat. Since not everyone in the unit could go there were sometimes drawings or competitions to select the lucky ones. Sometimes the competitions were based on body counts: The soldier who was credited with the most kills was rewarded with a ticket to the show.

Top. At Da Nang on June 20, 1966, Private First Class Stephen Mirales of the 2/9 Marines, 3d Marine Division, shows John Wayne how to sight in an 81MM mortar.

Right. Charlton Heston visits with Company F, 2d Battalion, 2/9 Marines, on January 20, 1966.

Opposite. The Bob Hope Show at Cam Ranh Bay, Christmas, 1968.

Top. Men of the 1/4 Marines, 3d Marine Division, watch a traveling song-and-dance troupe at Cua Viet on the coast just south of the DMZ.

Right, A cyclo race at Disneyland East, An Khe, 1966.

Opposite. A "boom-boom room" at Disneyland East.

It was difficult to avoid the USO shows. It seemed that everyone in the world who had an act got it together and brought it to Vietnam. Filipino go-go dancers, Japanese rock groups, standup comics—they all played Vietnam. Paid and transported by the U.S. government and virtually guaranteed an audience, the acts would troop from the officers' clubs of Saigon to the smallest outposts. Since the audiences were almost exclusively male, the most popular acts were the ones with the prettiest women.

For many veterans the Vietnam experience wouldn't have been complete without a visit to a "boom-boom room." These establishments were found in every village, town, and city that was handy to the Americans and their money. If there was no village near an American camp, a brothel would soon be created. The broth-

els were thinly disguised as steam baths and massage parlors or operated as annexes to bars and restaurants. Venereal disease was rampant.

In An Khe there was "Disneyland East," a miniature village built by the 1st Air Cav for its troops. According to photographer Marv Wolf, as soon as the Cav arrived, the once-sleepy village of An Khe was transformed into a "Southeast Asian version of a Bret Harte mining camp. Brothels, bars, laundries, restaurants, and souvenir shops sprang up literally overnight. There was no effective force for law and order. Armed American and South Vietnamese troops roamed the town drinking, wenching, and fighting. Cavalrymen returning unharmed from weeks of searching savage jungles for fierce Vietcong were shot, stabbed, blown up by 'friendly' hand grenades, or in-

fected by even friendlier microbes of the venereal sort."

Finally the commanding general of the Cav closed the town but had a new one built for his troops, closer to the base and tightly controlled. It was surrounded by barbed wire and guarded by MPs and Vietnamese police.

To gain entry a GI had to show his pass, dog tags, ID card—and medical shot record. Inside were row upon row of "boom-boom rooms," staffed, says Wolf, with "prostitutes who were checked weekly for VD by Army medics. After a decent introduction—five minutes, say—a GI retired to the back cribs with his choice of the available women. The sex was standard-priced, almost sanitary, semipublic, and awful."

Vietnam: People and Places

Rice fields in Binh Dinh Province, 1965.

Americans in Vietnam referred to the United States—or just about any place outside Vietnam—as "The World," thereby consigning Vietnam to another realm, alien and unwanted. It did have an other-worldly quality to most of the Americans who served there. Everything, from the landscape to the language, was different from what they had known in Maine or Iowa or Georgia or California. The cities were different; so were the farms, the weather, the food, the animals (water buffalo and tigers!), the religions, and the customs. There were different smells in the air, and even the sounds, such as the "bonk-bonk" and wail of Asian music, were strange and unsettling.

The Americans were not there as tourists and their movements through the country were not voyages of discovery; nonetheless they were struck by the varied beauty of Vietnam from its white sand beaches to its rugged mountains. Within the country is a wide variety of terrain from steep mountains to steamy swampland, each type with its unique vegetation—from triple-canopy jungle to plains of undulating elephant grass. Set upon this landscape are low, pastel-colored cities and Shangri-la hamlets with necklaces of emerald rice fields.

The old people seemed as ancient as Asia itself; the young were beautiful and delicate; the children were irresistible. Their way of life seemed timeless and elemental. At some level we were all affected by the beauty and the culture and wondered what it would be like without the war.

Opposite above. A village on the Thach Han River south of Quang Tri.

Opposite below. Scenes of Saigon: left, a bar girl and, right, a food stall.

Left. Balloon seller, Vung Tau, 1968.

71

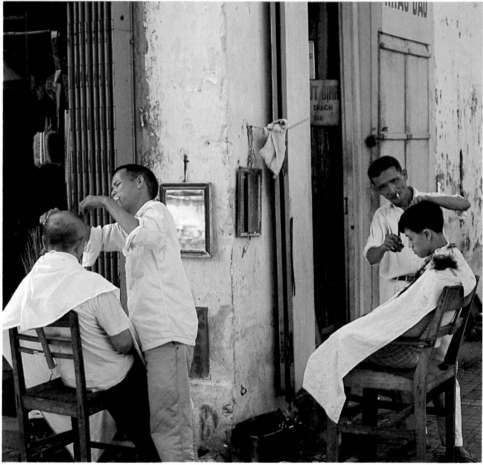

Town and Country

by Doug Clifford,

When I went to Vietnam in 1968, I had already been looking at vivid images of the war for over three years—since 1965, which was the year I realized that I was going to be drafted. It was then that Vietnam became a reality to me. By the time my brother John went there in 1966, as a grunt in the 3d Marines, Vietnam had become a part of the daily reality for my whole family. My mother kept scrapbooks of newspaper and magazine clippings and whenever I was home, my brothers and my mother had endless questions about what news I might have from the war and from John. So we watched as McNamara explained the bombings, and as Johnson reviewed the troops and visited the wounded. The daily papers showed us endless scenes of troops in combat, as well as shots of unfortunate civilian victims. We caught glimpses of life in the bush, along perimeters, in the rear, in and out of helicopters. We glimpsed operations undertaken in tremendous heat, in unfamiliar, strange terrain. We saw soldiers: young, very young, black, white, Hispanic, happy, sad, hurt, afraid, laughing, crying, going to and coming from Vietnam.

Sometimes we saw Vietnamese in these pictures. We saw them shuffling down the road, carrying their belongings or, if they were affluent, pulling a two-wheeled cart. I could not conceive that these people might be farmers, shopkeepers, barbers, mothers, uncles, or teen-agers, whose homes and businesses we had just destroyed. It never occurred to me that these people had jobs, families, problems, rent to pay, and property to maintain. We got to see the chief of police in Saigon blow out the brains of a captured Vietcong whose hands were manacled behind his back, but we never got to see a mother putting the rice on to cook for supper.

Opposite, clockwise from top: shanties on the backwater of the Saigon River; sidewalk barbers in Saigon, 1966; a schoolgirl strolls down a street in Qui Nhon in 1969.

When I got to Vietnam I saw many of the images that were not provided through media or military sources. I still recall clearly a scene from my first day in the country. We had flown to the coastal city of Qui Nhon from Cam Ranh Bay, and those of us who were headed elsewhere (to Phu Cat air base where I had been assigned, and to other places inland) had to find our own transportation. Without much trouble we found a truck and an agreeable army driver who was going our way. Beyond the base and past the edge of town the countryside became farmland. Hills rose in the distance, beyond the rice fields. The heat was striking in its intensity but bearable because of the breeze we felt on the back of the truck. Even through the haze the verdant green of the fields was beautiful. Occasionally we saw small houses beside the road and people working in the fields. At one point, under some trees by the side of the road, a small stand, like a farm stand, had been assembled. At the stand, behind wooden crates, were two small boys, perhaps six or eight, selling Orange Crush and Coca-Cola in bottles displayed in rows and piled on top of each other in small pyramids. We passed by and shortly they were gone from sight.

Momentarily I was stunned. Here I was in Vietnam, in a war, headed toward my duty station not knowing what to expect, and kids were selling soft drinks by the side of the road while the grown-ups worked the fields. There was obviously some kind of hoax going on. All of a sudden I felt as if I were in a parade and the beautiful scenery was part of the decorous route that had been set out for us.

The irony of that brief encounter never left me while I was there, and it is with me still. Evidently, whatever mission I was on was not shared by those I saw around their homes and fields, tending their wares. There are many sophisticated explanations for the scenes I witnessed on that first day, but none have cut through the reality of what I experienced then. Vietnam was, and is, a land of peasants. That day I saw people trying to feed themselves but managing to do so only on a subsistence level. And people who are hungry are not worried about communism or Communists.

During the year I spent in Vietnam I saw the Vietnamese more and more as

people with families. The places where they lived were homes and they had jobs. Some of them were farmers, and some were not. Sometimes they related to each other as friends, other times they didn't seem to like each other. This was the reality to which I was drawn. I wanted to take pictures of little children looking like children. I wanted to show the beauty of the landscape. The pictures I took of the people and their country were intended to be positive and to help people at home understand a little more about the Vietnamese people and the country that was—and still is—Vietnam.

Air Force Staff Sergeant Doug Clifford was stationed at Phu Cat air base from September 1968 to September 1969, processing and printing reconnaissance photography with the 460th Reconnaissance Technical Wing. He is now a teacher at Bunker Hill Community College in Charlestown, Massachusetts.

Doug Clifford at Qui Nhon, 1969.

Above. Civilians from a village on Barrier Island, southeast of Da Nang, are marched to a beach for evacuation during Operation Daring Rebel in May 1969.

Right. Villagers of An Binh are photographed on May 12, 1969, as part of the Phoenix Program, which attempted to identify and eliminate the infrastructure of the Vietcong.

Opposite. After having been rounded up, the entire population of a village near Bien Hoa listens to anti-Communist propaganda.

Civilians are the eternal pawns of war, pushed and pulled and brutalized by armies that claim to fight in their name, "the people." The civilians of South Vietnam were especially unfortunate. Two rival armies, the ARVN and the VC/NVA, were operating on the same ground, both demanding the civilians' money, produce, loyalty, and draft-age sons. The third army, the Americans, did not tax them or draft them, but neither did the Americans understand the Vietnamese and so treated them clumsily, contemptuously, and sometimes brutally. Entire villages were uprooted from their ancestral homes and moved into compounds where they could be better defended. Civilians were often caught in murderous crossfires between the opposing armies, and they were sometimes unceremoniously slaughtered by one side or other, in retribution for the sins of the enemy.

The people were affected in more subtle ways as well. Bedazzled by the wealth of the Americans, the Vietnamese sent young women into prostitution. Black marketeering and narcotics dealing became growth industries.

The Americans had great difficulty dealing with the Vietnamese because of linguistic and cultural barriers. There was also the problem of whom to trust, which the Americans solved by trusting no one. They learned that the ranks of the enemy included women, children, and even South Vietnamese soldiers.

Still the Vietnamese-American relationship had its moments of friendship, happiness, and even love. There were countless examples of cooperation and mutual trust, of assistance gladly given and gratefully received. The Americans, many of them barely out of boyhood, were captivated by Vietnamese children and enchanted by the delicate, exotic beauty of the young women. In the hurly-burly of war, boy managed somehow to meet girl. A number of these romances led to marriage.

The protracted acquaintance of the Vietnamese and the Americans spanned the octaves of human emotion. The low notes were discordant and jarring; the highs were the sweet notes of understanding, brotherhood, and love.

It must have been extremely hard at times for the Vietnamese to understand that the Americans were trying to help. The villagers could be herded at gunpoint from place to place, subjected to gross indignities, and treated as less than human. They were frightened by the war and by the methods of the soldiers from the other side of the world. Civilians were injured and often killed, sometimes deliberately.

Opposite above. A Vietnamese family takes shelter in a ditch during a firefight between a unit of the 101st Airborne and the enemy in 1969.

Opposite below. A woman kneels over the body of her son, who was killed when the Vietcong rocketed and mortared her village to punish the residents for cooperating with the South Vietnamese forces, 1968.

Above. A Vietnamese civilian pleads with the 101st Air Cavalry Division soldier who is interrogating him during a search and destroy operation in early 1968.

Somehow the Vietnamese managed to cling to the essential dignity of their centuries-old culture, as George Denoncourt, a combat photographer with the 1st and 5th infantry divisions, remembers:

"They are a very polite and gracious people. They were bewildered; they did not know what was right; they were at the mercy of whomsoever had power over them at the moment. Their lives were governed by the season, by agriculture, the water buffalo. The simplicity of their life-style, the lack of anything material, made their nobility stand out. They went about their business in a kind of holding pattern, while we went about our business all around them.

"It must be terrible not to have any vista, any ability to plan your future, any idea of what is going to happen. They couldn't function the way a Vietnamese community is supposed to—the pecking order, for instance: The lowly barber is suddenly rich and becomes a leading figure in town because all the GIs get haircuts."

Opposite. This South Vietnamese man changed into his best clothes to pose for an American photographer in a village near Phu Cat in 1968.

Above. Civilian war casualties recovering from their injuries at a rehabilitation center in Saigon, 1968. Many American military doctors performed volunteer work at centers such as this.

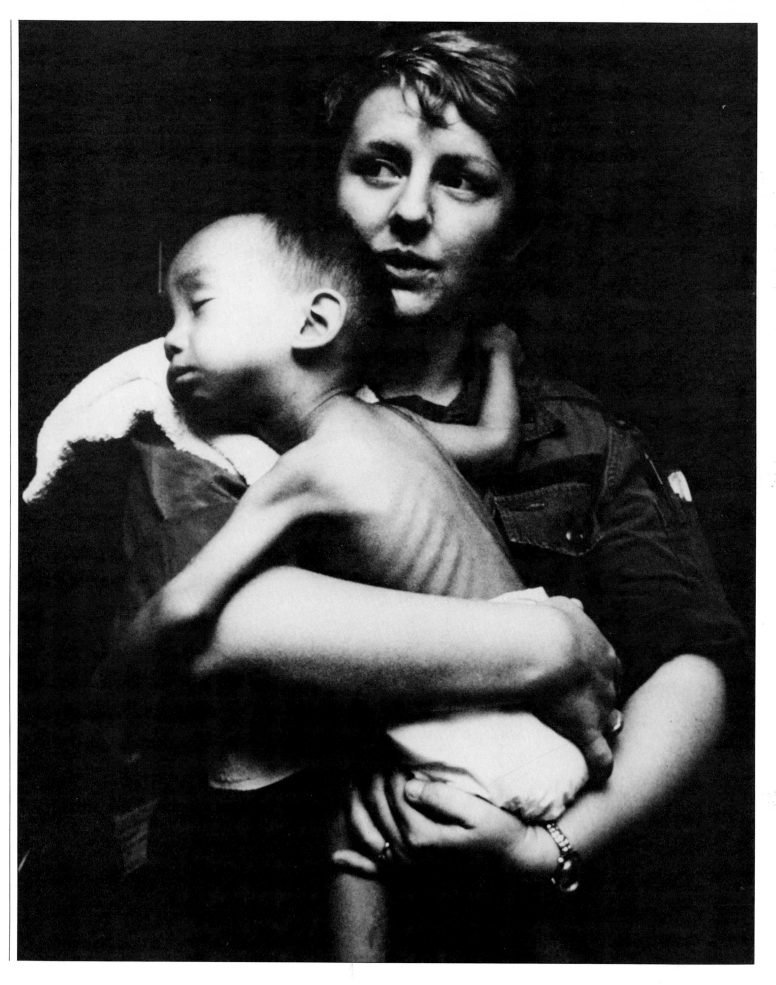

Opposite. An American nurse holds a dying Vietnamese child at the army hospital at Long Binh, 1968.

Left. A medic of the 1st Air Cavalry carries a wounded child to a landing zone to be evacuated to a hospital during Operation Pershing in the An Lao Valley, 1967.

81

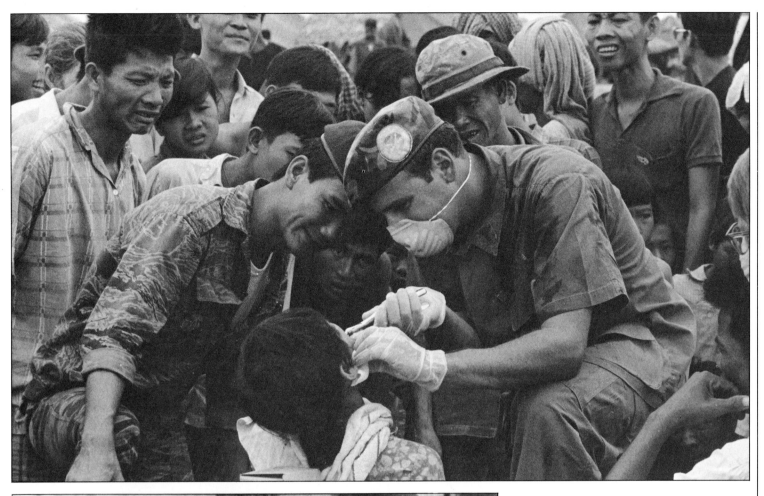

The Americans did bring many forms of nonmilitary help to the South Vietnamese and for a time, at least, it bettered the lot of some of the people. Perhaps the most successful of the "people to people" efforts were the medical assistance programs. The Americans stopped epidemics of malaria, vaccinated entire communities against diseases, and applied modern medicines and drugs to cure the sick and heal the injured.

It was a novel experience for the American medical people. A routine tooth-pulling was a community event.

Medical help was extended to the chickens, too.

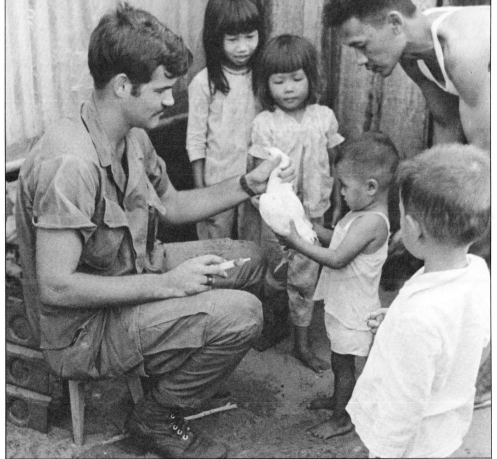

Opposite. An infantry officer of the 1st Infantry Division hands out treats to children in Lai Khe, north of Saigon.

Above. Dr. (Captain) Arthur Goldberg has an audience as he pulls the tooth of a Mekong Delta villager on July 6, 1970.

Left. Gunner's Mate David Muxen demonstrates how to inoculate chickens against disease.

Opposite. U.S. soldiers spend some time with refugee children, 1968.

Above. Chief Hospital Corpsman Stephen Brown, 1st Marine Division, talks with two young boys at a refugee camp in Quang Nam Province on November 1, 1970.

The small children were beautiful. Their innocence was all too soon sacrificed by a war that recruited them as grade-school grenade throwers and prepubescent riflemen. But the Americans' hearts went out to the children, and the children responded. The war brought about many touching, transient encounters between the big Americans and the littlest Vietnamese.

Above. Children in the Phong Dien refugee camp northwest of Hue in early 1967.

Right. In a village southwest of Saigon, a young boy poses proudly beside an American APC in mid–1968.

Above. Montagnard children at a refugee camp at Dak To in July 1969.

Left. The child of a black American soldier and a Vietnamese woman in Saigon, 1969. Such children—and their mothers—were often discriminated against by the South Vietnamese.

In Combat

Company E, 2/3 Marines, in close combat on Mutter's Ridge near the demilitarized zone during Operation Lancaster II, 1968.

Combat is the dark, brutal heart of war, where soldiers come face to face on the killing ground. Combat is the maker of heroes and cowards and all colors of character in between; it has been called man's ultimate experience. Certainly it is an experience no man forgets. Combat is noisy, confusing, and scary, exhilarating and terrifying at the same time. Combat in Vietnam seemed to hold an extra measure of fear and confusion because it was so often fought at close quarters in dense vegetation with a frequently invisible enemy. Air and artillery support were often not only difficult but downright hazardous; many American casualties were the result of misdirected "friendly fire."

Photographing combat is a taxing assignment. It's just about impossible to photograph an infantry battle, except perhaps from the air, and even then not much would appear to be happening. Since combat is such a close, intense event the photographer does best to focus on the actions of individuals or small groups of soldiers and on their faces where the true story of war can be seen. Through it all the combat photographer is exposed to the same risks as the combat soldier and more than once has had to put down his camera and fight.

———————

Much has been written about the big battles of the Vietnam War—the 1968 Tet battles of Saigon and Hue, the siege of Khe Sanh, the fight for Hamburger Hill. But those were exceptional in Vietnam. Day to day the war was fought by small groups of soldiers in small places, nameless battlegrounds where the fighting was very close, intense, and deadly. Bob Hodierne's photographs of a Bravo Company firefight in the Hiep Duc Valley in

Opposite. A soldier of Bravo Company, 4/31 Infantry, Americal Division, runs for cover as his unit comes under NVA fire in the Hiep Duc Valley northwest of Chu Lai.

Left. A Bravo Company squad leader hits the dirt, yelling commands.

A Weary Company Fights On With Rifles, Grenades, Guts

By SPEC 4 BOB HODIERNE
S&S Staff Correspondent

HIEP DUC VALLEY, Vietnam—The fighting here is a very close, personal, infantry fight.

The valley bottom is dried terraces, each terrace three or four feet higher or lower than the one next to it. Around each of these tiny fields are thick hedgerows. And in the middle of the hedgerows are ditches and bunkers— ditches and bunkers that you just know Charlie is in.

Bravo Company, 4th Battalion, 31st Infantry, Americal Division, knows it. They were here when it all started last week and have been chewed up and chewed up again until Thursday morning they numbered only seventy–three men and two officers.

Thursday evening, when the fighting was over, they would number only forty–six men and one officer.

Thursday morning Bravo Company moved slowly forward—forward being the direction they had to move—to join Marines fighting from the other end of the valley. The Marines were just a few hundred meters ahead and everyone hoped this time they might find nothing in between.

At eleven A.M., two machine guns, two AK47 [sic] and an M79 grenade launcher blew that hope away.

Pinned down in the late morning sun, a very hot sun, Bravo had a man killed, a new guy, and thirteen others wounded or nearly unconscious as a result of the heat. Heat that sometimes reaches 120 degrees.

Carefully they pulled back, leaving the body of the new guy, to evacuate their wounded.

By two P.M. the sixty – one men of Bravo Company were ready to move back into the same area. No one really wanted to go. They just wanted to sit in the shade and be left alone.

The commander, Captain William H. Gayler, explained the situation. There would be no helicopter gunship support. The gunships had more important things to do than support Bravo Company. Air and artillery couldn't be used because the Marines were too close. They had no mortars. The infantryman, with his rifle and grenade, was expected to dig out the North Vietnamese.

Wearily, Bravo moved forward again—only to be pinned down almost at once.

Low crawling ahead, the first fifteen men were cut off from the rest of the company. Men who had been tired for days, men with no water, men who were really scared, were on their own.

The man nearest the cut off group was told to carry grenades forward to them. He refused,

crawled back and asked the medic for pills for his nerves. While hiding back with the wounded, the nervous soldier was wounded by an M79 grenade round fired by the NVA.

While the rest of the company lay pinned down and helpless, the point group fought it out with Charlie. Late in the afternoon, just as darkness was coming, the point men managed to escape, crawling a few meters back to the rest of the company.

Four more Americans were dead — their bodies still forward.

The company threw out tear gas and looking like monsters in their gas masks, tried to advance against the enemy to recover the bodies. They managed to get just one of them. Five more NVA were dead and two captured M60 machine guns destroyed.

As night fell, the company straggled back to find a place to sleep.

Friday morning, more tired than Thursday morning, but now only forty – seven strong, Bravo knew they would have to go back in to get the bodies.

late August 1969 show this kind of warfare. Hodierne was a Specialist 4 on assignment for *Pacific Stars & Stripes* when he took the pictures, and his story of the fighting—reprinted here—was later attacked by a high-ranking USARV officer as "treason."

A few days after Hodierne's story appeared in *Stars & Stripes*, Colonel James Campbell, chief spokesman for the U.S. Army Command in Vietnam, sharply criticized Hodierne's use of U.S. casualty figures and his references to the company pulling back, to its fatigue and unwillingness to advance, and to the lack of air

Opposite above. The enemy—close and dug in—pins down Bravo Company.

Opposite below. Hodierne's account of the Hiep Duc battle as it appeared in Stars and Stripes *on August 31, 1969.*

Above. A Bravo trooper throws a grenade.

Left. Crawling through the low grass, the GI directly behind Hodierne was killed by a sniper.

Above. Captain William H. Gayler of Bravo Company and his men contemplate their situation, knowing that they must move forward once again and try to overcome the NVA force.

Opposite. Bravo Company carefully pulled back to evacuate their wounded and dead. Here, a trooper comforts a dying buddy.

support. Colonel Campbell told the Associated Press: "It is the opinion of USARV that such stories do not border on treason—they are treason" and "devastating to the morale . . . of all soldiers . . . [and] of tremendous aid and comfort to the enemy."

But Bob Hodierne never had doubts about his job as a photojournalist, and he believed his duty was to tell the story as he saw it. He had been told by *Stars & Stripes* managing editor John K. Baker to act as a civilian reporter even though he was in uniform. Hodierne did, and the result was outstanding photojournalism.

Later Hodierne told a *New York Times* reporter that Pat Luminello, the *Stars & Stripes* Saigon bureau chief, had said the military command wanted to see only "pap" in *Stars & Stripes*. When the quote appeared in the *Times*, Luminello (a civilian) was fired and Baker (also a civilian) resigned.

Opposite. The door-gunner of a navy heli-copter gunship readies for a firing run over a Vietcong ambush site in the Mekong Delta. The burning river patrol boat has just been hit by recoilless-rifle fire.

Above. River boats were lightly armored and vulnerable to enemy fire. A navy assault support boat has been damaged by enemy fire forcing the crew to beach the sinking craft.

Combat in Vietnam frequently involved a combination of the elements of warfare. Air support, infantry, artillery, and sea power might all work together in a single battle. The infantry routinely received air and artillery support, and if the battle was within range of naval guns another element could be added. The huge sixteen-inch guns of the battleship U.S.S. *New Jersey*, among other ships, frequently joined the fray, and the ship's computer-assisted guns were reputed to be more accurate than many land-based artillery batteries. And, of course, a prime example of integrated military operations was the use of tactical air support from carrier-based aircraft. There were very few purely naval battles or aerial dog-fights in Vietnam. Except for North Vietnam's sophisticated air-defense system, the U.S. and South Vietnam enjoyed domination of the air and the sea.

The rivers posed a different problem, for although a river patrol might be a navy operation it was really more of a waterborne infantry or armor patrol. Attacks almost invariably came from shore, and the river boats would frequently put troops ashore and then support them with firepower. The rivers were highways where the army, navy, marines, air force, and Coast Guard all worked together.

Above. Lieutenant Commander Donald Sheppard aims a flaming arrow at a bamboo hut concealing a fortified Vietcong bunker on the Bassac River, November 1967. The longbow was part of the boat's equipment, carried for just such a purpose.

Right. The machine gunner of a navy river patrol boat returns enemy fire in the Mekong Delta in January 1968.

On December 19, 1968, the first of two heli-copters carrying SEAL Team 1 approaches the village that will be the target of their surprise raid.

The navy's Seal (Sea, Air, and Land) teams are an elite force of highly trained commandos skilled in underwater, air-borne, and ground combat. In Vietnam, they carried out a variety of exotic and usually classified missions. Seal Chip Maury photographed this operation in December of 1968 as Seal Team 1 carried

out a surprise daylight raid on a village on the Cua Lon River in Vietcong-controlled territory on the Ca Mau Peninsula. The objectives were to capture and bring back for interrogation as many civilians as could be found and to destroy any structures being used by the VC.

The operation was carried out under

Above. The SEAL team begins its assault.

Right. Two SEALs fire at VC positions across the Cua Lon River.

fire from several armed VC who had fled into the woods at the approach of the helicopters. While part of the team returned and suppressed the VC fire, the other Seals raced through the small settlement, rounding up the women, children, and old men and herding them to the LZ. The huts were burned, documents

Above. After setting fire to the hut, a team member carries away a bag of Vietcong documents that he had found inside of it.

Left. A boy who had been hiding from the SEALs in a canal is captured for interrogation.

Above. Pinned down by enemy fire, a machine gunner opens up on the enemy while his platoon's demolitions expert, at left, seems stunned.

Opposite. Wounded twice by enemy fire, the machine gunner lurches forward across his M60.

It is a rare occasion that a combat photographer captures the moment when a soldier is hit by enemy fire. Specialist 4 James Lohr photographed such a moment while serving as a photographer with the 101st Airborne Division, Bravo Company, 2d Battalion, 502d Infantry, during Operation Benton west of Chu Lai. They were pinned down by an enemy force, and Lohr took these remarkable shots of the action.

The other remarkable fact about these pictures is that they survived at all. Jim Lohr explains: "After the GI was wounded we were overrun by the VC. During our escape we were crossing a river and all of my equipment went under water several times, as did myself. We had two more soldiers wounded while crossing the river." Back at Chu Lai Lohr developed the film, expecting it would be totally ruined. But the images had sur-

vived the dunking in Vietnamese river water, except for a few water stains which, if anything, added to the drama of the pictures.

Another of Lohr's experiences, also during Operation Benton, underscores one of the problems of being a combat photographer: He was expected to be a soldier first. Lohr was with a patrol pinned down by VC automatic weapons fire. One trooper who tried to advance on the enemy position was wounded, and repeated attempts to reach him failed. Finally Lohr put down his cameras and crawled to the wounded soldier, but too late—he was dead. Photographer Lohr took a grenade from the dead trooper and managed to kill one enemy soldier and put the rest to flight. Jim Lohr was decorated with a Bronze Star for his bravery.

The job of the infantry is to move forward, to attack, whether it means crossing an open field, inching up a battle-scarred hill, or penetrating the thick jungles where visibility was only a yard or two.

Opposite above. A marine of Company M, 3/4 Marines, moves out on the double with a 3.5 inch mortar round during Operation Prairie near the DMZ, September 30, 1966.

Opposite below. Troopers of the 173d Airborne Brigade charge across an open field toward Vietcong positions, in War Zone D, 1967.

Above. Ninth Infantry Division troops return fire in thick cover in the Mekong Delta, 1968.

Left. A 1st Air Cavalry soldier lets fly with a grenade during fighting at LZ Baldy near An Khe in 1968.

The first rule of ground combat is "Keep your ass down." Stay low and get whatever you can between yourself and the guys who are shooting at you. Marine combat correspondent Tom Bartlett recalls the time the Da Nang Press Center came under small arms fire. The officer in charge, Colonel Tom Fields, and a civilian took refuge behind a wooden crate. "You realize, of course," the colonel muttered to the civilian, "that if this crate is filled with corn flakes we are in a world of trouble." When enemy rounds are coming in, there's no such thing as too much cover.

———

Right. Trooper of Company A, 2/502 Infantry, 101st Airborne, in an old Vietcong trench defends an artillery battery against a VC assault near Kontum on June 7, 1966.

Below. For one 9th Infantry Division soldier, getting pinned down means lunch break.

Wounded

by Frank Lee

It was on the afternoon of the seventeenth of March 1967, when I joined the 1st Platoon, Lima Company, 3/4 Marines, 3d Marine Division, commanded by Lieutenant O'Sullivan. We took off at approximately 1500 hours from the Dong Ha airstrip in CH-46 helicopters and landed in the rice fields near the village of Gio Do. Our mission, the lieutenant informed me, was to sweep the village and an adjacent hamlet, which the VC had supposedly been through earlier that morning.

No contact was made in the village, but when we started sweeping the second hamlet, sniper fire opened up and was followed by automatic weapons fire. Everyone dived into the small depressions beside the road and in the bushes. I recall Lt. O'Sullivan jumping across a barbed-wire fence and running to see where the heavy firing was coming from. After reloading my camera, I ran along a small ditch, jumped over the fence, and caught up with the lieutenant. The firing had slackened and O'Sullivan ordered his left flanks to move up again on line.

Sniper fire began again as we began crossing a dry rice field, and by the time we had reached the middle of the field we spotted a VC about seventy-five meters to our right rear. The lieutenant took a grenade, slowly maneuvered himself toward the enemy, and tossed a grenade into the sniper's hole. Heavy firing continued as he ran back to my position, but his action destroyed the enemy position, killing the VC.

We continued for about twenty meters, when the enemy again opened up on us with machine guns. They had us in a crossfire. O'Sullivan, the point man, the radioman, and a rifleman were pinned down near a bush line paralleling us. I was pinned down about fifteen meters from them but managed to continue filming.

Soon our machine gunner's ammunition was nearly exhausted and then he was hit. He slumped over and Lt. O'Sullivan grabbed the machine gun and returned fire. Then his radioman was shot through the stomach. The lieutenant yelled to me to relay more ammo but a marine fifty meters from me couldn't understand me. I waved to him to join us and he ran across a stretch of open field and manned the machine gun. I stopped filming and crawled over to the wounded radioman and opened his jacket with my knife, but I could only apply a bandage to his wound to try to slow the bleeding. Then I helped him crawl past the machine gunner and directed him along a ditch that led away from the enemy fire and told him to crawl to a thatched hut nearby. Lt. O'Sullivan started to regroup his men in the ditch, and I crawled back with my camera and bag.

I filmed a few more scenes as the fire grew more intense, and I believe the lieutenant was hit at this time. I assumed we were still in the enemy's open field of fire so I continued to crawl toward the thatched hut. An enemy gunner walked his rounds in on me, one bullet piercing my canteen, then another ricocheting off the earth and hitting me in the forehead. I lay still, hoping the enemy would assume he had killed me, then yelled to one of the men in the hut to cover me as I ran for the hut. Inside were the wounded radioman, our forward air controller, and another radioman. Through an opening in the hut I could see the VC moving to our right flanks with automatic weapons, trying to envelop us.

I yelled to Lt. O'Sullivan, who was trapped in the ditch with the wounded and dead twenty-five meters from the hut. I tried to relay his orders to the marines to position themselves back on line and establish a perimeter defense, but the heavy firing kept them from doing so.

The radioman called for reinforcements and gave our situation report to battalion. The FAC tried to call in helicopter gunships but didn't want to take the chance without knowing where all our men were. I told him I would observe and went around the rear of the hut to make sure from the lieutenant where all the men were. He replied that all the men were behind us and to do whatever was necessary. I suggested calling in air support and asked the lieutenant to pop smoke and then have the gunships make a trial run. The first strafing run was slightly off. We called for correction and the subsequent runs were on target. The enemy was approximately fifty meters in front of the lieutenant's position.

After the firing runs by the gunships, the enemy fire subsided, but from the hut I could see more VC coming from the front. I warned the lieutenant to anticipate another attack. Battalion headquarters called and advised us that Kilo Company was coming out to reinforce us and that we would be a blocking force for their sweep. I told the radioman to advise battalion that we had heavy casualties and I didn't think we could hold as a blocking force. Our flanks were completely pinned down.

Then a corporal arrived at the hut and took charge of the remnant of our platoon. He called Kilo Company and asked them to give position reports. Our platoon was scattered, and with darkness coming on our positions couldn't be determined visually. The men started yelling, "Kilo!" in the darkness to make sure the reinforcements wouldn't fire on them.

At about 1930 hours, Kilo Company approached our lines and we directed them to our positions. At this time we were able to get Lieutenant O'Sullivan and the dead and wounded marines out of their position where they had been pinned down for so long.

In the field in 1967, Frank Lee signals for a roll of film.

Marine Sergeant Frank Lee served as a combat correspondent in Vietnam from November 1966 to December 1967. He is now an account executive with a publishers' representative in Los Angeles. For his actions during the battle he describes here, Sgt. Lee was awarded the Bronze Star for valor.

Khe Sanh was not the only siege of the war, just the best known. In June and July of 1969, Bob Hodierne covered the siege of Ben Het, a small Special Forces outpost ten kilometers from the borders of Laos and Cambodia. The base was under heavy NVA artillery fire and did not have enough manpower to fight off the enemy. Since it was in territory defended by ARVN troops, all the base could do was hold on and wait for ARVN reinforce-

Above. The defenders take cover as mortar rounds hit the Ben Het Special Forces outpost in June 1969.

Right. The Special Forces captain commanding the base watches his ammo dump blow up after it took a direct hit from a rocket.

Opposite. A smoke screen is laid down to shield the area inside the camp where supplies were air dropped. The smoke protected the soldiers sent to retrieve the supplies.

ments. But the ARVN infantry seemed reluctant to fight their way over twelve kilometers of road to reach the little base, and the defenders had to rely on U.S. air and artillery support to beat back the constant threat of a large-scale ground attack. In the end, help never did arrive. The NVA simply ended the siege and declared a victory, claiming the battle of Ben Het had shown the "Vietnamization" policy to be a failure.

Above. A Special Forces captain at Ben Het gets more bad news after the ammo dump was blown up: Bad weather will prevent resupply anytime soon.

Opposite. A Ben Het defender shows the stress of days of steady bombardment.

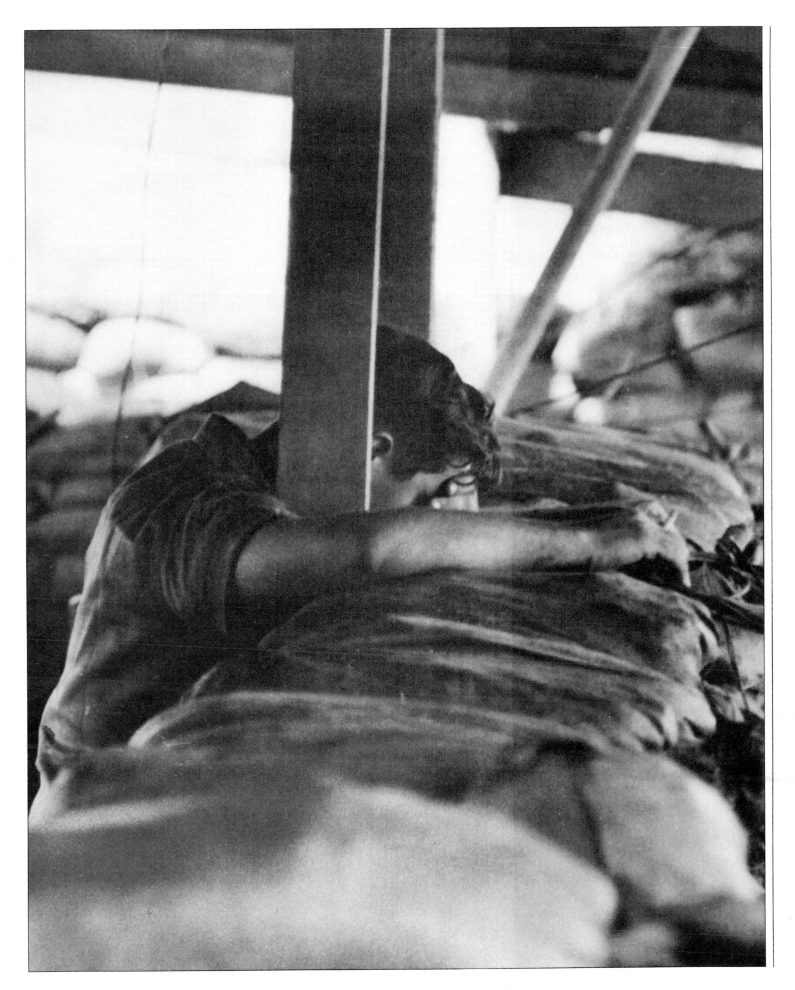

Marines rush a badly wounded man to a medevac helicopter after he was injured by a booby trap sixteen kilometers northeast of An Hoa on January 21, 1969.

Medical evacuation, the medevac—one of the many missions of the helicopter in Vietnam—saved untold numbers of American lives. The medevac crews were among the best trained and most dedicated military units in Vietnam and frequently risked their lives to land under fire and evacuate wounded soldiers.

On a Medevac Mission

by Doug Woods

Two marine grunts blasted by RPG rounds are picked up northwest of An Hoa. Both are carried onto the chopper in blood-filled, dirty poncho liners. Both men lie shattered, yet alive. The first has his right arm missing below the elbow, his right leg gone below the knee. Blood-soaked bandages and tourniquets squeeze the pressure points.

The second marine is worse. His legs and arms are gone. A bone dangles grotesquely from his left shoulder, shreds of muscle and flesh drooping lifeless from the bone. The upper part of his skull is also shot away, exposing hemorrhaging flesh and dripping brain matter around the inadequate battle dressing. Incredibly he lives.

I have seen blood and gore before, but previously the worst medevacs were dead, the live ones in recognizable shape. I offer to help the corpsman on these two, but he impatiently waves me away. So I retreat to my red plastic perch to hold a plasma bottle dripping solution into the hose that stabbed the second marine's shoulder. I watch intently as Doc feverishly works on the first grunt.

The second man lies at my feet, his blood spattering my flight suit as it sloshes back and forth on the poncho. Suddenly, the marine's eyes open and roll in their sunken sockets; in an instant they seem to focus on me. Our eyes meet. Oh God! I want to run and hide and be sick, but I cannot move. Frozen in fear by this man's gaze, I stare back into his glassy eyes. He betrays no emotion, no pain, no real awareness of his condition. I reason that

Doug Woods in Da Nang, between missions, 1969.

shock and morphine are keeping him so quiet and still.

I steel myself against feeling sorrow or compassion for this marine, who is no older than myself. Like the rest of the chopper's crew, I know I must stifle my emotions or I may lose control. And losing control is something that must *never* happen in combat. Inside me I want to cry, but I suppress the feeling. Finally, I kneel down at the grunt's side and force a weak smile. He shifts his eyes from mine and, raising his bloody body a little, he looks down and over at where his arms and legs used to be. I look too. At the same time I wish in my heart that this brave man will die. I am not proud of myself. He looks too mutilated and shattered. He should be dead. So why isn't he dead? I ask myself. He lays his head back down and our eyes meet again. I nod to him.

I see no response, but he knows! He has to know.

He looks away from me, his unblinking eyes staring at the CH-46's ceiling. The visual connection broken, I stand and carefully move forward a little, away from his penetrating gaze. I am careful not to yank the intravenous needle from his shoulder.

I try not to stare, but again and again I am drawn back to the shattered men near me. I feel utterly useless. Hopelessness and anger pervade my thoughts. I am terribly uncomfortable. I suddenly hate flying. I hate the war. At this very moment these two marines lie on the verge of dying. And for what? They are facing the ultimate reality of war; who gives a damn about war photographs or dispatches? I want the flight to end quickly so these two medevacs will be gone and things can get back to normal for me.

Soon they disappear from my sight. But to this day they linger in my consciousness.

I do not know whether the two grunts lived or died. I pray they lived . . . especially the second marine. That's because I could have been him.

Corporal Doug Woods served as a Marine Corps combat correspondent based at the Marble Mountain Air Facility near Da Nang in 1969 and 1970. He is now a mortgage loan officer at a bank in Portland, Oregon.

The availability of helicopters for evacuation of the wounded meant that most casualties were only minutes away from a well-equipped field hospital or a floating hospital off the coast. Of course, sometimes it took a lot longer. On days of heavy fighting you could scream for a dust-off until you were blue in the face, but a chopper could only be in one place at one time. And there were times when the enemy had a lot to say about the speed and success of a dust-off mission.

The wounded were flown to well-equipped field hospitals or to hospital ships off shore.

Right. Navy Corpsman Joe Gruszkiewicz checks the tag of a wounded marine while in flight to the Naval Support Activity Hospital in Da Nang, August 12, 1970. The marine was wounded by a booby trap southwest of the city.

Opposite above. A wounded marine struggles to speak through a radio while a corpsman holds the radio and an intravenous fluid bottle, 1967.

Opposite below. A surgical team on a navy hospital ship removes shrapnel from a badly wounded marine.

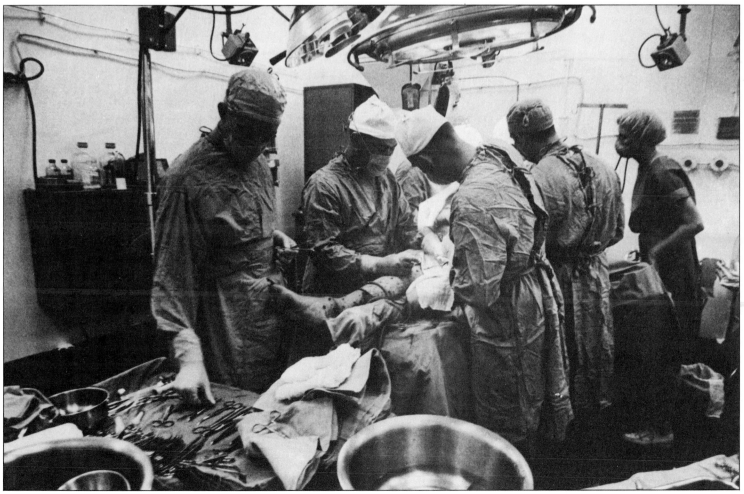

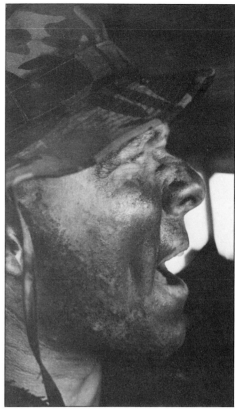

Above. A SEAL yells "take-off" as the helicopter comes under sniper fire.

Left. Captured civilians aboard the helicopter.

Following pages. After the mission, SEAL Team 1 shows off a VC flag captured in the village. Photographer Chip Maury is in the back row at far right.

and a VC flag were seized, the choppers were called in, and the team took off, still under fire but with no casualties. The entire raid had taken only minutes. The civilians were flown to Hai Yen, then taken aboard a navy ship for interrogation. They were finally taken to a resettlement camp in a government-controlled area. Several of the civilians said they had been kidnaped by the VC and put to work in the rice fields in the little village where the Seal Team had found them.

Opposite. A helicopter arrives to lift out the SEAL team and the villagers it captured.

The most terrible sights of the war were the dead, but the wounded were the hardest to photograph. Taking a picture of a wounded soldier seemed such a callous response to the human suffering. Surprisingly many of the wounded seemed to welcome having their picture taken and took it either as an expression of caring or as an indication that they had achieved a certain celebrity status, however dubious.

Opposite. Corporal Isaiah Martin comforts his scout dog, wounded by a VC bullet in the Que Son Mountains on May 30, 1970. Corporal Martin is a scout for Company M, 3/7 Marines, 1st Marine Division.

Above. Medic George Pigmtora, Company B, 2/7 Cavalry, 1st Air Cav, applies pressure to his chest wound as he waits to be evacuated. He was wounded during Operation Masher near Bong Son on January 25, 1966.

A medic checks the intravenous bottle (above) for a trooper (right) injured by a VC grenade in a tunnel near Nui Ba Den.

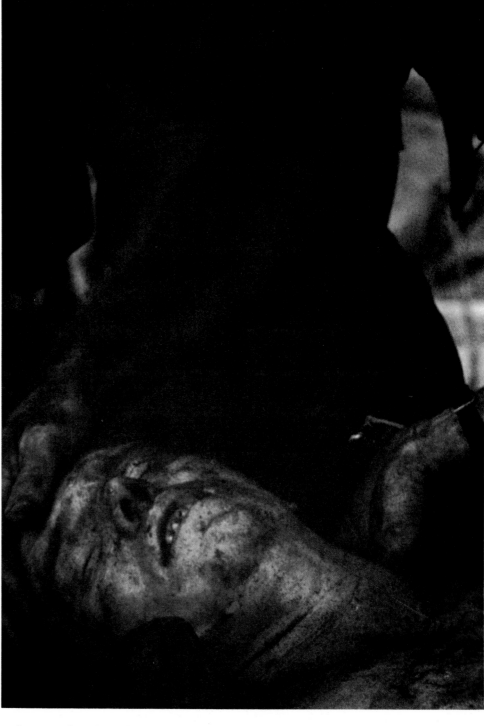

During Operation Cliffdweller IV in early 1970, units of the 25th Infantry Division were conducting reconnaissance-in-force down the boulder-strewn slopes of the Black Virgin Mountain, Nui Ba Den, near Tay Ninh. Combat photographer First Lieutenant Don Critchfield and his team from the 221st Signal Company were with two companies of the 3d Battalion, 22d Infantry, 1st Brigade, 25th Infantry Division. Critchfield recalls: "The boulder field is on the east-northeast side of the mountain and begins about one-third of the way up the mountain. At the base of a saddle formed by the smaller Nui Cau is a sort of boulder-strewn amphitheater. The VC, having gotten there first, got all the good seats." The companies descended past the boulder fields without incident, but after they had gone by, the VC came out of their hiding places among the boulders and began firing down on the troops, touching off several firefights. After the enemy had been driven off, one soldier was investigating one of the natural tunnel complexes in the boulder field. He encountered an enemy soldier, who shouted, "*Chieu hoi,*" as if he were going to surrender. The American didn't shoot—and the VC threw a grenade at him. His buddies pulled him out and began treatment while waiting for a medevac chopper. (See pictures, this page.)

Sometimes the Vietnam War burst out of the jungles and into the cities, as in the 1968 Tet offensive, which was launched the night of January 30. The worst of the urban fighting was in Saigon and Hue,

Opposite. During the Tet offensive in February 1968, marines scale a mound of rubble that was once the east gate tower of the Citadel of Hue.

122

Above. A marine takes a cautious look from a window during heavy fighting in Hue.

Right. A marine wounded during Tet is dragged to safety with his M16.

Opposite. Wounded and dead marines are evacuated by tank from Hue. (This photograph won the Robert Capa Award of the Overseas Press Club.)

and army Specialist 4 John Olson covered the action in both cities for *Stars & Stripes*. For his memorable photos, some of them shown on these pages, Olson was given the Robert Capa Award by the Overseas Press Club. Hue was the only city held by the Communists during the Tet offensive. But, after nearly a month of fighting, U.S. and South Vietnamese forces finally retook the old imperial capital, in the process turning whole sections of it into rubble.

While all the attacks were eventually quelled—and perhaps as many as 72,000 Communist troops killed—the vulnerability of South Vietnam to such an attack in light of official U.S. optimism about the war made an unprecedented number of Americans question U.S. involvement in Vietnam.

A Picture Is Worth . . .

by Nick Mills

Nick Mills in the central highlands, 1969.

It was February 26, 1969, and the beginning of the Communists' post-Tet offensive. We were in house-to-house fighting in a village just outside the big Bien Hoa air base. ARVN and U.S. units had trapped a large combined NVA/VC force, which apparently planned to attack the air base. The enemy was hiding in the village refugee center. I had been sent there with my photo team by the SEAPC commander, Major Jim Carson, early in the morning as the battle was beginning. For most of the morning we stayed with the ARVN Rangers and their U.S. adviser as they tried several unsuccessful assaults on the dug-in force. At noon I drove back to Long Binh and requested more photo teams, because after gunships and bombers had softened up the place there was apparently going to be a tough ground battle.

Combat photographers Dwight Carter and Howard Nuernberger came with me. Two other photo teams from SEAPC were also covering the action with motion-picture and still cameras. Major Carson even left his office to join the effort and coordinate the teams.

In midafternoon the ARVN assault began in earnest. As we moved into the village with the ARVN we saw enemy soldiers emerge from hiding places and surrender; the bodies of others lay here and there. It was hot, very loud, dusty, smoky, and confusing. Carter, Nuernberger, and I split up with different elements of the assault force as the Rangers advanced under heavy fire. The ARVN were beginning to take casualties. An American photographer was killed and Carter helped carry his body out. Suddenly, the noise level jumped dramatically as the enemy counterattacked. We were pinned down by machine-gun and small arms fire, and the boom of enemy rocket-propelled grenades rose above the din. The ARVN pulled back in a hurry, dragging their dead and wounded. I pulled out with them, hoping aloud I wouldn't be hit as we sprinted across a flat, open area that led to safety. I made it to the shelter of a large building that served as the ARVN command post. There I began looking for my team. Behind the building I found a cluster of SEAPC photographers and Major Carson huddled over a prone figure on the ground. The man obviously was an American, but his face was bloody and blackened, his uniform was in shreds, and his right arm was missing just below the shoulder. A stick of white jagged bone jutted from the bloody stump of the arm. I had to ask who it was. "Nuernberger," was the answer.

Howard! A tall, lean, quiet kid from Pennsylvania; a fine, sensitive photographer, and one of my favorite people in the 221st Signal Company. He, Carter, and I had just returned from Chu Lai where we had spent two weeks photographing American Division operations and waiting for the anticipated offensive.

Now he was unrecognizable to me. He had been in a doorway in the village when the counterattack came and he had taken a direct hit by an RPG. The doorway shielded all but his arm from the blast; otherwise he would have been dead. As it was his face was powder-burned and bleeding, his uniform was torn from head to foot, and there was that obscene stump of an arm. He was alive, however, and conscious, and able to talk. Now I had to get him out of there.

A few yards away a U.S. adviser worked a radio, yelling for a dust-off. But none came; they were busy elsewhere. We wrapped Howard's stump to stem the bleeding and waited for a medevac chopper. I screamed at the adviser, he yelled at the radio, but there was no chopper available. One hundred yards away I spotted a group of ARVN ambulances, waiting to evacuate their casualties over land, and I decided that they were our best hope. Surely the ARVN would give us a lift to the Long Binh hospital. We got a litter and put Howard on it. Four of us then carried him to the ARVN ambulance trucks and tried to put him on one. The driver shook his head no. He smiled, but he would *not* give the wounded American a ride. ARVN only.

I couldn't believe it. This ambulance driver was refusing to take a wounded American to a hospital? In my mind I saw the enormous irony of the situation: It was 1969, there were a half-million Americans in Vietnam fighting so the Vietnamese could eat their rice in peace, and this son-of-a-bitch wouldn't give us a ride to a hospital to save this man's life.

In addition to my camera I was carrying an M16, and the ambulance driver suddenly was seeing the business end of it. I ordered Howard loaded aboard the ambulance, put Carter on with him, and told the driver to take Howard to the 21st Evac Hospital on Long Binh Post or we'd kill him. I meant it. Carter kept his rifle at the ready but I had convinced the driver. In fifteen minutes Howard was in surgery.

I stayed at the battle a while longer, until the air strikes had softened up the village and the ARVN began mopping up. I then pulled out and headed for the hospital. When I arrived Howard was still in surgery, but the doctors had finished their work and the OR team was putting the final dressing on Howard's injury. I waited in the ward where he would be placed, among rows of other badly wounded GIs. The OR doors swung open and the surgeon, still in his scrub suit, strode out, peeling off his bloody rubber gloves. He came straight to me.

"Are you that man's commanding officer?" he demanded. I said that I was and asked about Howard. "How is he? What the hell do you mean, how is he? He's lost an arm, that's how he is!" I was startled at the man's anger. He was a major, an army surgeon in Vietnam, and surely he had seen cases as bad, and worse. But he was furious—spluttering, screaming, furious—and his anger was directed at me. "Can you justify that, lieutenant?" he yelled. "Can you justify that? Losing an arm to take a goddamned picture? Can you?"

I was too stunned to answer. I said nothing. The surgeon turned and stomped away, anger and disgust still contorting his face. Then Howard was wheeled out, the stump of his arm encased in clean, white bandages. He was still awake, and I sat by his bed for a while, not knowing what to say to him, either. I told him he was a good man and I was very sorry this had happened, to which he nodded. Finally I left; next day Howard was flown out of Vietnam.

By the time I got back to SEAPC headquarters the surgeon's anger was raging inside me and I made something of a scene, slamming my steel pot against a wall and yelling obscenities about the war and our part in it. A few nights later, I was told, I went to pieces while very drunk, screaming and crying about Howard and the war and our mission; to this day I have no recollection of it.

Long after I returned from Vietnam, during one of countless mental replays of the Bien Hoa battle, it suddenly occurred to me that the surgeon who had been so angry didn't understand that we were only doing our jobs: He had not understood that we were combat photographers, and our jobs were as relevant and justifiable—or as irrelevant and unjustifiable—as anyone's in Vietnam.

[Note: Howard Nuernberger returned to the Pittsburgh area and runs the public affairs office of the Pittsburgh Plate Glass Corporation, where his duties include photography.]

Top. During the battle near Bien Hoa in February 1969, a rocket-blasted hole in the wall of a home provides a jagged frame for the ARVN Rangers trying to dislodge a well-entrenched NVA force.

Bottom. An ARVN Ranger, hit in the throat by an enemy bullet, is carried from the battle.

Above and right. Soldiers of Company A, 2/3 Infantry, 199th Light Infantry Brigade, drag a sampan from a canal in the "Pineapple Region" southwest of Saigon on July 23, 1968, after sinking the sampan and killing three VC who were trying to escape from the unit's cordon and search operation. Two other VC were captured and two escaped.

Fire is both a weapon and a by-product of war. From the "rockets' red glare" to the burning of huts to the awesome cone of fire from the "Spooky" gunships, at any hour of the day or night there was fire from one end of Vietnam to the other. As spectacular in action as they were deadly, the AC–47 and AC–130 gunships,

Above. Marines of Company D, 1/26 Marines, burn Vietcong huts in Quang Tri Province during a search and destroy mission in August 1966.

Left. A guard tower is silhouetted against the flames of an ARVN fuel depot in Qui Nhon after it was hit by VC mortars on August 12, 1969.

Left. "Puff the Magic Dragon," the AC-130 gunship, fires its Gatling guns.

Above. As the gunner aims through a Starlight scope, tracer bullets fired from his AC-130 gunship appear as abstract art in a time exposure taken from inside the aircraft.

nicknamed "Puff the Magic Dragon" or "Spooky," left a deep impression on all who saw them in action. Former combat photographer Chris Bunge of the USAF 600th Photo Squadron remembers his Spooky missions in 1969:

"We flew out of Thailand aboard AC-130A gunships, equipped with both 50MM and 16MM Gatling guns. We flew over the Ho Chi Minh Trail. The photo mission was to photograph the almost unbelievable kill record of these aircraft. We photographed through Starlight scopes and attempted to show on film each destroyed truck.

"I will never forget the experience, flying totally blacked out, circling targets invisible to the unaided eye; then the sudden roar, the red fire and sparks pouring from the guns. Explosions dotted the earth below, then antiaircraft fire from three batteries seeming to drift slowly up toward us. The antiaircraft observers aboard would follow the flight of the rounds and call in triplets to the pilot, "accurate . . . accurate . . . inaccurate," as they saw that the rounds would miss their target—us. The pilot stayed on course until he heard three "accurates" crackle into his headset, then took evasive action. I can recall hearing the sizzle of a tracer round as it passed near my camera position.

"Every night we would fly over the trail, coming home in the early morning hours and turning in our film—which I never saw again—then off to bed.

"Thailand was green and peaceful and aromatic. The contrast between the night combat and the next day, sitting by the swimming pool in bright sunshine with an iced drink, was awesome."

My Lai

Above. Company C lands just outside My Lai to begin the assault.

Opposite. My Lai villagers about to be shot by U.S. troops. As Haeberle walked away after taking this picture, several GIs opened up with their M16s and shot these people.

Sergeant Ronald L. Haeberle became the best-known—or most notorious—of all the military photographers who served in Vietnam. He also became the most widely published, all because of one roll of film—the pictures he shot of the slaughter of civilians in the hamlet of My Lai 4 on March 16, 1968. When those pictures were published more than a year after the massacre they lifted the lid off a story which had been gradually coming to light and helped set the stage for the most sensational war crimes trial in American history. The photographs showed the public the darkest aspect of the U.S. involvement in Vietnam; the pictures also tarnished the image of Americans who fought in Vietnam.

Ron Haeberle was not a trained army photographer. He was functioning as an army photographer in Vietnam at his own initiative. Haeberle was drafted into the army in 1966 and, after training, became a mortarman. He was assigned to the 11th Infantry Brigade at Schofield Barracks, Hawaii, where he began putting his hobby of photography to official use. "They didn't have a Public Information Office when I arrived," recalls Haeberle, "so I more or less started one." When the 11th Brigade was shipped to Vietnam in December 1967 Haeberle was established in the unit's PIO, which had grown to seven enlisted men and three officers. The brigade became an element of the 23d Infantry Division—the Americal—which had been activated in September 1967.

The brigade was based at Duc Pho in southern I Corps, an area in which the Vietcong were numerous and had many sympathizers. The 11th Brigade began conducting search and destroy missions in the area around Duc Pho. Sometimes the units would make contact with the enemy, but more often they would not and the principal hazards they encountered were mines and booby traps. Haeberle

Above. A man and two young boys, shot down by GIs as Haeberle watched.

Right. Haeberle remembers that when the American troops fired at these two little boys, "the older one fell on the little one as if to protect him. Then the guys finished them off."

Opposite. The Americans set fire to the hamlet, burning everything they could, including bodies of the villagers.

joined the infantry units on some of these operations but didn't see any real combat action. "The hostile fire I saw was mainly on night guard duty, when the VC would probe the perimeter," says Haeberle.

In March of 1968, Ron Haeberle was preparing to go home. He had arrived in Vietnam with just four months left to serve in the army. (Although one year was a normal tour of duty in Vietnam for army personnel, because the 11th Brigade shipped over as a unit there were many soldiers, like Haeberle, who arrived in Vietnam with less than a year left to serve.) He still had not been in combat. On March 15, he was offered a chance. The PIO was notified there would be a battalion-size operation the next day aimed at destroying the 48th VC Local Force Battalion, which was believed to be located in Son My, a village with a cluster of subhamlets including the village designated as My Lai 4. Haeberle volunteered to photograph the operation. Specialist 5 Jay Roberts, one of the combat reporters in the 11th Brigade PIO, also volunteered.

"I heard it was supposed to be a big deal," says Haeberle, "and I thought, 'I really gotta see some heavy combat, see what it's all about.'"

The massacre

As was usual when he went into the field, Haeberle was carrying two 35MM cameras. One was his army-issued Leica, which was loaded with black and white film; the other was his personal Nikon which was loaded with color slide film.

"We went in on the second wave of choppers," he recalled, "about 7:30 in the morning. We jumped off the chopper and heard a bunch of gunfire. I thought there was something really going on in the village. I couldn't see anybody in the village because the rice was fairly high and there were trees. So I went with a group of soldiers down toward a trail. I then saw people—Vietnamese—walking down the trail and these guys just started opening up on these people. But there was no return fire.

"I wondered what was going on,"

Haeberle continued, "I'd seen Vietnamese people with their goods on their back, you know, that's their normal way of going to market in the morning, and all of a sudden the GIs open up on them. When we got to the bodies we could see they were nothing but civilians. I started to take pictures.

"Then I was actually walking next to a GI and he found an old man and two kids on the trail, and the kids were really scared. The American GIs were supposed to be buddy, friend, and that. And this GI just mowed them down! That really started to get to me, and I looked at this guy and said, 'What the hell are you doing?' and he just mumbled something and shrugged it off and kept going."

That was the beginning of it. For four hours Ron Haeberle and Jay Roberts stayed with the troops at My Lai. Only once did the GIs seem at all concerned about the presence of Haeberle's camera. That was when he came upon a group of GIs and a cluster of civilians, four women and three children, huddled by a small

Bodies of Vietnamese civilians—men, women, and children—litter a road leading into My Lai.

stand of bamboo trees. The youngest of the women was buttoning up her blouse. GIs had been trying to rip off her clothes, but one of the older women had fought the soldiers off. When a GI noticed Haeberle's camera he yelled "Whoa, whoa!" whether to caution the photographer or the other GIs is not clear. Haeberle took a picture of the civilians, then turned and started walking away. "All of a sudden 'Bam, bam, bam, bam!' and I look around and there's all these people going down."

Haeberle estimates that he witnessed directly the killings of at least fifty Vietnamese at My Lai, including a number of small children. The shooting of the children, he says, really bothered him. But by the end of the morning he and Roberts were still trying to figure out what had happened. Haeberle said later he wasn't sure if he had witnessed a war crime or if this kind of thing happened on every operation. It was his first big combat operation; they had been told there would be no one in the village but Vietcong, and, he says, "You hear a lot of stories about little kids carrying grenades, kids who are booby trapped, stuff like that." And the GIs didn't seem hopped-up or wild,

they were calm and methodical, as if they knew just what they were supposed to do.

Shortly before noon, Haeberle and Roberts boarded a helicopter and returned to Duc Pho. Haeberle turned in the black and white film he had shot at My Lai—two or three rolls of 35mm film—and put the roll of color slide film he had shot into his duffel bag to take home with him. He and Roberts talked about what they had seen. After a couple of days they agreed the best thing would be to say nothing.

Spec. 5 Roberts, instead of writing about what he really saw at My Lai, wrote an account of the operation for the brigade newsletter that carefully avoided any mention of civilian deaths. Haeberle's black and white pictures were tossed into a desk drawer in the brigade PIO, where they remained for months. Two weeks after the massacre, Haeberle left Vietnam, and the army.

When he got home Haeberle processed all the color film he had shot in Vietnam and put together a slide show of his military career. Included were the pictures of the massacre.

At first he showed the slides only to

friends, but then he began to get invitations to show the slides to groups—the Kiwanis, the Rotary Club, high school groups. "Reactions were mixed. There were some people," recalls Haeberle, "who actually looked at the pictures on the screen in front of them and said 'This couldn't happen. No, this didn't happen.' One person asked me if I shot them in a studio. There were also some people who said that this ought to be brought out, that the pictures should be published, but I showed the slides for quite awhile and nothing ever came of it."

The investigation

More than a year after the My Lai massacre, on April 4, 1969, Ron Ridenhour, a former 11th Brigade soldier, mailed thirty copies of a letter he had written, detailing what information he had gleaned about the massacre from his conversations with GIs who had been there. Nine copies were mailed to President Nixon, others went to members of Congress, the Pentagon, and the State Department. A number of congressmen who received the letter pressed the army for an explanation, and the investigation began. Investigators began tracking down the men, many of them civilians by then, who had been in My Lai. Many of the men were vague in their accounts of the day and seemed to have difficulty recalling the events of March 16, 1968. On August 25, 1969, the investigators found Haeberle.

Haeberle says when the Criminal Investigation Division (CID) men came to see him, they talked for eight or ten hours one day and a couple more hours the next day. The CID men told him that as many as 500 civilians had been killed.

Haeberle gave them copies of his slides. (He keeps the originals in a bank vault.) He also told them about the black and white pictures, which the investigators later found in the 11th Brigade PIO. Armed with the photographs the investigators returned to requestion the other soldiers. "From my understanding," says Haeberle, "the photographs brought everything back to them about what happened there. Finally they had some real concrete evidence."

In early September of 1969 the army made public the fact that Lieutenant William Calley (who had been in command of the platoon that did much of the killing)

was being detained for possible court martial on charges of murder, but nothing was said about the basis for the charges. Still, it was enough to spark press interest in the story. On November 13, some thirty newspapers carried a story about the massacre written by Seymour Hersch, based on interviews with some of the soldiers who were there. Four days later the *New York Times* published a front-page story with interviews of Vietnamese survivors of the massacre. On November 18, Ron Haeberle called Joseph Eszterhas, a former high school friend who was a reporter for the Cleveland *Plain Dealer*, and two days later Haeberle's story and photographs were published in the *Plain Dealer*. Later Eszterhas, acting as Haeberle's agent, sold the publication rights to Haeberle's pictures to *Life* magazine.

The official military inquiry into My Lai, headed by Lieutenant General William Peers, accused Haeberle of suppressing evidence of war crimes, something of which the other men who were at My Lai that day were also accused. All were members of the same unit and no one, including Ron Haeberle, had wanted to break silence and get the others in trouble. Though he turned in his black and white film to the brigade PIO, he doubted that such pictures would be published by the Americal Division.

The Peers inquiry also concluded that Haeberle "may have wrongfully appropriated and disposed of photographs taken as an army photographer . . . ," referring to the color film Haeberle took home and later sold to *Life*. General Peers's final report also noted that, "There appears to be no clear policy regarding the ownership and release [U.S. Army versus individual] of film exposed by army photographers using personal cameras while on official missions." The military investigators urged the army to set forth guidelines for the future. This was being done even before the Peers report was issued; after the My Lai photographs were published the army began a major effort to establish stricter guidelines for photographers so that no film shot during an official mission could be considered the personal property of the photographer.

"We were all part of it."

Haeberle is plain spoken and direct, but there is a reserve, a coolness about

him, and a lack of emotion even when talking about witnessing the murders of Vietnamese children. It "really got" to him, he said several years after the incident but added that he never experienced any psychological problems—no nightmares, no depression—from what he saw at My Lai, even the dead babies and children.

When asked about the money he has made from the My Lai pictures, Haeberle shrugs and says he had "made a few bucks here and there." *Life* still owns the rights to the pictures, and each time one of the pictures is published—for a fee as high as $300.00 for one-time use—Haeberle is paid a percentage. Haeberle says it was never his intention to make money from the pictures and he made no attempt to sell them until the My Lai story broke. Even then, he says, it was at Eszterhas's urging that he sold the rights to *Life*.

Haeberle was called to testify before the Peers panel, and he also testified at the trials of Lieutenant William Calley and Captain Ernest Medina. Haeberle feels it was wrong to put those men on trial without also trying every other individual who saw or participated in the massacre at My Lai. "We were all part of it. I was like an accessory to the fact, if they want to call it murder. Every GI there was." But Haeberle says he never felt compelled to tell higher authorities about the massacre, then or later. "Maybe," he says, "if I understood what had happened in the ditch, and the body count. But at the time I didn't know about the ditch where all the bodies were.

"To me it was hard to rationalize, like, is that part of war? I mean, it may be the first time you see something like that, and what are you going to think. You don't know until you're there. You don't know until you experience it."

A few months after the big 1968 Tet offensive, the enemy regrouped and launched a second offensive in May, which became known as "Tet II." Although Tet II was neither as well planned nor as damaging as the first, it involved 119 attacks throughout the country. Saigon once again proved a major battle ground and fighting there continued off and on into June. The neighborhood around the "Y" Bridge, a three-pronged overpass that linked Saigon with the Mekong Delta, and Saigon's Chinese district of Cholon were scenes of some of the heaviest fighting.

Opposite above and left. Troops of Company B, 2/47 Infantry, 9th Infantry Division, move against a well-entrenched enemy force near the "Y" Bridge on May 11, 1968.

Opposite below. In the Cholon section of Saigon during "Tet II" in May 1968, an explosion turns a former Shell gas station sign into an ironic comment on the war.

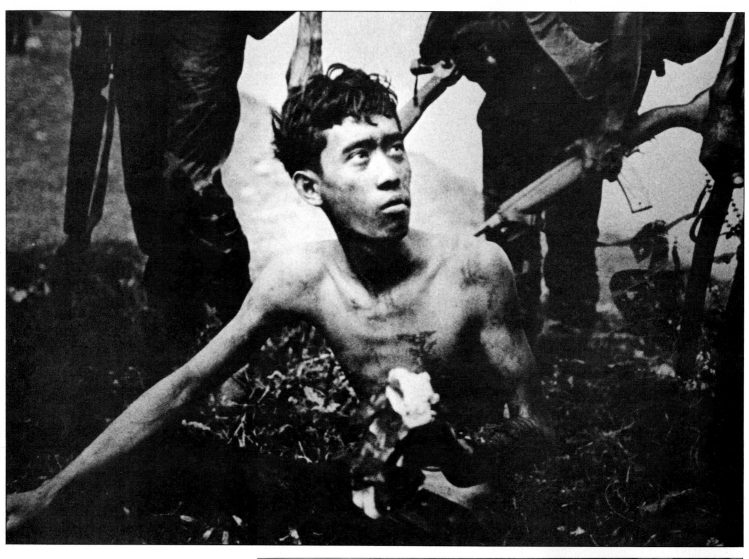

Above. A soldier of the 9th NVA Division is captured while fighting in the French National Cemetery in Saigon during the second Tet attack.

Right. A Vietcong prisoner awaits interrogation on January 23, 1967, at the U.S. Special Forces Camp at Thuong Duc, twenty-five kilometers west of Da Nang.

Opposite above. Vietcong suspects are transported by a tank crew of the 1st Battalion, 26th Marines, during Operation Daring Rebel in May 1969.

Both sides took many prisoners in the long course of the war; some people believe to this day the Vietnamese still hold U.S. prisoners of war. There were many stories of cruelty and brutality in the treatment of POWs by both sides, stories that must have evoked mixed feelings—relief at being alive and terror at being a prisoner—in those who were captured.

Above. A rifleman of Company A, 1/20 Infantry, 11th Infantry Brigade, leads a VC suspect to LZ Liz in Southern I Corps for interrogation on July 3, 1969.

Right. Members of the 1st Air Cavalry and their Vietnamese interpreter (wearing shoulder patch) use water torture on a Vietcong prisoner, 1968.

Opposite above. During the New Year's Day, 1969, prisoner release, the POWs, left to right Specialists 4 James W. Brigham and Thomas N. Jones and Private First Class Donald G. Smith, wait for the formalities to finish before they are released to the American side.

Opposite below. American Master Sergeants Pitzer and Johnson are held in a Vietcong POW camp in the U Minh Forest.

At the end of 1968 the National Liberation Front announced it would free three American POWs as a goodwill gesture. First Lieutenant Joseph Tourtelot, of the 221st Signal Company, was assigned to photograph the release. On January 1, 1969, the unarmed Americans flew to the release site near the Cambodian border. Lt. Tourtelot later recalled the American POWs appeared quiet and worn and did not show much emotion. After reciting a prepared statement to the POWs, the NLF signed them over to the U.S. officers and they were flown to the hospital at Long Binh Post. (One of the POWs, SP4 James W. Brigham, died in a U.S. hospital shortly after his release, of complications from a head wound that had been treated by his captors.)

Above. A medic of the 173d Airborne Brigade tags a body for evacuation on November 23, 1967, after an assault during the battle for Hill 875 southwest of Dak To.

Right. ARVN soldiers killed by Vietcong on March 13, 1963, in the Plain of Reeds, thirty kilometers southwest of Saigon.

Death is the ultimate obscenity of war. Most of the Americans who fought in Vietnam were of an age when men believe that death is a long way off. Vietnam quickly taught them otherwise. The inevitability of death was forced upon them, to be carried with them from that time on. They had of course seen death in their lives, but it had been death from illness, age, or accident, the kinds of death to which young men feel they are immune. There was no such feeling in war. In fact, it sometimes seemed that survival was a matter of chance.

Above. Soldiers of the 1st Air Cavalry killed these enemy soldiers in a night ambush. The next day the ambush squad was ordered to bury the bodies, but they found the ground too hard to dig so they simply piled up the bodies and walked away.

After the battle you wiped away the mud and the blood, took out your dead and wounded, let the emotions come out, and began to think about the next time.

Above. An artillery forward observer and his radio-telephone operator of the 2/60 Infantry, 9th Infantry Division, take a breather after a battle in the Mekong Delta in 1969.

Right. After a firefight, the mud of a rice field covers a soldier of the 2/60 Infantry, 9th Infantry Division.

An officer of the 101st Airborne Division breaks down as he tries to radio for helicopters to evacuate his company's casualties after a battle in 1966.

Opposite. A radioman comforts a buddy of Company A, 2/7 Cavalry, 1st Air Cav, after a battle during Operation Byrd in Binh Thuan Province on August 26, 1966. Nearly all of his platoon was killed during the fight.

Above. A soldier of the 5th Infantry Division (Mechanized) looks out across the fog-shrouded A Shau Valley, 1969.

Good-byes

All aboard the freedom bird! The 9th Infantry Division goes home.

In 1969 a new word joined the lexicon of the U.S. military in Vietnam: Vietnamization. What it meant was that in the ensuing three years the Americans would turn the war over to the Vietnamese. The Vietnamese would be given the guns, the planes, the helicopters, the ammo, and the money—and the Americans would pack their duffels, board the "freedom birds," and go home. Vietnamization meant we would eventually declare South Vietnam's military ready to take over the whole job, whether or not it really was, and, in effect, hand the South Vietnamese the keys to the war. Three years after being put in the driver's seat South Vietnam's forces were pushed into the sea by the North Vietnamese juggernaut.

Many of the Americans left with curiously mixed emotions. Almost everyone who served in Vietnam counted the days until they could go home. So there was relief, of course, as the freedom bird cleared the coastline and climbed steadily out of reach of the war. But there was sadness over the buddies who had died and anxiety about what was waiting at home when a man, changed by a year in Vietnam, renewed his relationships with family and friends who were changed by a year in America without him. And there was more psychological baggage carried by many—survivor's guilt and a huge emptiness at saying good-bye to the most intense experience of their lives.

Opposite. Men of the 3d Battalion, 9th Infantry Division, at farewell ceremonies for the division on July 8, 1969, at Tan Son Nhut air base.

Left. General Creighton Abrams, commander of U.S. forces in Vietnam, prepares to encase the colors of the "Big Red One"— the 1st Infantry Division—at the division's farewell ceremonies at Di An, ten kilometers north of Saigon, on April 3, 1970.

Opposite. U.S. Navy sailors lower the American flag for the final time on September 10, 1971, at the U.S. camp at Thuan An, twenty-five kilometers northwest of Hue. The base is being turned over to the South Vietnamese navy.

Above. The 1st Division's colors are furled.

Left. Lieutenant Colonel H.L. Johnson, commanding officer of the 3/5 Marines, 1st Marine Division, holds the last round to be fired by the 105MM howitzer battery at Fire Support Base Ross on February 14, 1971.

Beginning in mid-1969, American units began pulling out of Vietnam. Most ended their service with some kind of ceremony. The men of the 3d Brigade of the 82d Airborne Division, one of the last American units to be deployed to Vietnam, left for home on December 11, 1969. Before they left, their commander, Brigadier General George W. Dickerson, told them:

"You've done a tremendous job here in the 3d Brigade, 82d Airborne. You fired over a third of a million rounds of ammo, and you've done untold damage. I don't think we'll ever really be able to evaluate just how much damage you've done, and how much you've done toward ending the war here in Vietnam. But one thing I'd like all of you to reflect on: I think each of us in our own way has to decide, what are we doing here in Vietnam, whether or not you're contributing or whether you're wasting your time. It's going to be something you'll have to wrestle with yourselves."

Opposite above. Paratroopers of the 3d Brigade, 82d Airborne Division, board C–141 aircraft for the flight to their stateside base, Fort Bragg, in North Carolina.

Opposite below. An officer addresses 82d Airborne troopers during the division's stand-down ceremonies at Phu Loi, northwest of Saigon.

Above. Vietnamese nuns wave farewell to a freedom bird at Tan Son Nhut air base.

Marine combat correspondent Frank Lee, who left Vietnam on December 7, 1967, remembers vividly the last moments of his tour of duty:

"Everything suddenly rushes up on you. It's time to go home! This place fills me with mixed emotions; happy because I'm going home yet painfully sad because I'm leaving a small group of friends I've shared a part of my life with. Anxiety hits me cyclically and, like jolts of electricity, reminds me I am going home. But the calm moments are also here, and memories, both happy and sad, stir the innermost grief.

"I am going. They are still here. And the beat goes on.

"The jets whine as the aircraft gains speed down Da Nang's water-soaked runway. Water splashes, reminding me the monsoon season has arrived. The raindrops hit the window and gently roll down, leaving a prismatic trail. Through the clouds our bird climbs until Vietnam disappears behind us, and above—sunshine! As bright as silver, and, even to us enclosed in our little microcosm high above earth, inviting, alive."

The Wounds Inside

by Leroy Massie

Leroy Massie shoots a noncombat job.

We went to Vietnam because our country sent us there. We did the job we were sent to do. Some of us experience disorders. I saw many of my friends killed in Vietnam. Each time I went on a combat mission with a different combat unit I would make friends with men in the unit. When you see friends shot up, blown up, and killed day and night it does something to your mind and you never forget the tears, blood, and death. These scenes live with you forever.

I have an emotional disorder that I cannot control sometimes: I have nightmares about the war in Vietnam. I am always being chased by the VC. I wake up sometimes sweating and screaming. I go through stages of acute depression. I cry when I see terrible war scenes about Vietnam. I cry sometimes when I see sad scenes on TV.

I take cover sometimes when I hear a loud noise. I cry sometimes when I think of all the brave soldiers I have seen wounded or killed in Vietnam, black and white. I know for a fact that I have been exposed to Agent Orange. I know that I experience post-traumatic stress disorder because of my Vietnam experience. I know I am trying to live a normal life despite the stress and depression I am experiencing. I do not talk about the things that are wrong with me because most people do not believe me. Although I look healthy, I am a sick man. I am not asking for sympathy, but with a little understanding from the outside world I will be able to make it. It will take hard work and strong faith in God and myself, but I will make it.

Sergeant First Class Leroy Massie was a motion picture cameraman for the Department of the Army Special Photo Office in Vietnam between 1964 and 1973. After retiring from the army he became a library technician at the Library of Congress in Washington, D.C.

Some of the Americans went home with their units, but many more left Vietnam alone and arrived home alone. Leaving Vietnam may have seemed like a happy event, but going home was often a difficult and disappointing experience. The transition from the field to one's hometown was abrupt. There were no welcoming parades; in fact for most returning Americans there was no one even to say "thanks." They encountered antiwar demonstrations in the streets; family and friends could not relate to their experience in Vietnam.

Above. An airman leaves Phu Cat air base on the first leg of his journey home, August 1969.

Left. Some soldiers volunteered for a second tour, but this trooper had no choice. He had just completed one tour with the 173d Airborne Brigade, and, when he returned home, had been assigned to the 82d Airborne Division at Fort Bragg, North Carolina. Just after he joined the 82d, the brigade was shipped to Vietnam in February 1968.

In 1973, after the last American combat forces had left, came the "peace with honor" the Nixon administration had sought. The Paris peace agreement was signed, the guns ceased firing, and the prisoners of war came home. In January of 1975, the North Vietnamese Army began the final assault that brought it total victory in four months. As the Communist army raced southward, South Vietnamese soldiers and civilians alike fled before it in panic and disarray. They fought and killed each other to get aboard planes and ships that would get them out of the country. After the fall of Saigon and the evacuation of the U.S. Embassy, American ships waited offshore to receive those refugees who found the means to reach them. For Americans, it was the final page of the story, the last pictures for the Vietnam album.

Opposite. Vietnamese refugees who have fled the final NVA assault in April 1975 cram the deck of the U.S. merchant ship Greenport. They await barges which will put them ashore on Phu Quoc Island in the Gulf of Thailand off Vietnam's western coast.

Above. A Vietnamese air force helicopter is ditched in the sea near the U.S.S. Blue Ridge on April 29, 1975, the day before South Vietnam surrendered. This is one of fifteen helicopters that landed aboard the Blue Ridge with escaping Vietnamese military personnel and families. The helicopters all had to be ditched because of a lack of space on deck.

Left. A little Vietnamese refugee inspects the boots of a U.S. Marine aboard the U.S.S. Durham in April 1975.

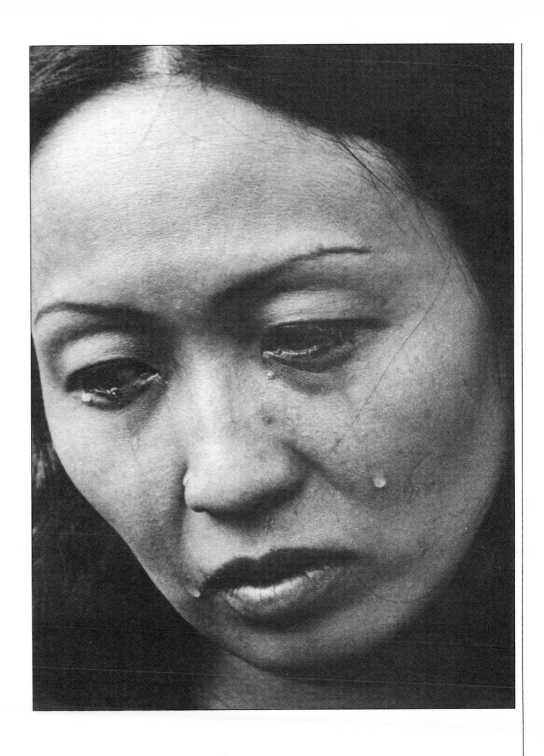

Opposite. The exodus of Vietnamese leaving their country continued long after the war was over. This boatload of Vietnamese refugees ties up alongside the U.S. Navy frigate U.S.S. Whipple *in August 1978.*

Above. A Vietnamese refugee arrives at Eglin Air Force Base in Florida in late 1975.

This is the legacy of war: Halfway around the world from her homeland, a land she will probably never see again, a refugee arrives, alone on a foreign shore. Her past is full of sorrow, her future full of uncertainty; yet, she is among the more fortunate of war victims, considering the plight of most of those who were left behind, or those who were wounded and disabled—or those who died.

Faces
of War

Navy SEAL Bud Gardner on a reconnaissance patrol in the Nam Cam Forest in the Mekong Delta.

The many faces of war reflect the wide range of experiences men had in Vietnam. Fear, fatigue, and resignation darken the faces of combat soldiers; prisoners of war glower in sullen defiance. Soldiers' faces also show pride, determination, and sometimes a newfound maturity, a matter-of-fact confidence from enduring hard times. There were good times, too, and strong camaraderie among the men who shared the Vietnam experience. Their faces tell the human side of the story.

Opposite. U.S. Marine Major Milton Cherne, a U.S. adviser in command of a helicopter unit, ferries ARVN troops into battle on the Plain of Reeds in the Mekong Delta in 1962.

Left. A trooper of the 1st Air Cavalry after a firefight, 1968.

Above. Four South Vietnamese marines share a moment of camaraderie near Quang Tri City in 1972.

Right. An ARVN trooper at Bac Lieu prepares to go on night partol in the central highlands in 1966.

Above. Navy crewmen of a river patrol boat of Task Force 116 in the Mekong Delta, 1968.

Left. Two GIs near Long Binh in 1968. Combat soldiers talked about not getting too close to their buddies, but they found there was no one else they could talk to who understood.

Above. A soldier of Company B, 4th Battalion, 31st Infantry, Americal Division, after a battle in the Hiep Duc Valley west of Chu Lai, 1969.

Above right. A VC captured by the 25th Infantry Division troops near Cu Chi in 1968.

Right. An American soldier with a VC skull, 1968.

A VC captured by ARVN soldiers in May 1962 has had her hands bound with her own flag.

Staff Sergeant Clarence Brown, Company L, 3/5 Marines, 1st Marine Division, takes time out for a smoke during Operation Meade River southwest of Da Nang in 1968.

A soldier of the 199th Light Infantry Brigade peers from behind the body of a soldier felled during a firefight southeast of Saigon in 1968.

The day's mission over, this helicopter door-gunner can relax for a few hours before it begins again: another day, a new mission, another risk.

A marine of the 26th Regiment, his face clouded by brooding uncertainty, heads south in a convoy on Highway 1 south of Da Nang in 1968.

Sources

Photographs:
Note: *With the exception of the pictures of Roger Fenton on page 7 and Mathew Brady on page 8, all photographs were taken by combat photographers serving in the U.S. military.*
Cover, SSG Shearer, U.S. Marine Corps. pp. 7, 8, The Bettman Archive. p. 10, Sp5 Leonidas Stanson, 221st Sig. Co., U.S. Army—collection of James Vick. p. 12, Cpl. Philip R. Boehme, U.S. Marine Corps. p. 14, JO1 James Randall, U.S. Navy. p. 15, PFC John Olson, 53d Sig. Bn., U.S. Army. p. 16, top, U.S. Army; bottom, 1LT Karel, U.S. Army. p. 17, left, PHC A. Hill, U.S. Navy; top right, Sp5 Leonidas Stanson, 221st Sig. Co., U.S. Army—collection of James Vick. p. 18, U.S. Army. p. 19, top, PFC Henry V. Backes, Jr., U.S. Army; bottom, Sp5 Darrell DuRall, 39th Sig. Bn., U.S. Army. p. 20, top, U.S. Navy; bottom, U.S. Army—*Pacific Stars & Stripes.* p. 21, top, Cpl. R.L. Pearson, U.S. Marine Corps; bottom, Sp4 James Pardue, U.S. Army. pp. 22-3, Sp4 George J. Denoncourt II, 1st Inf. Div., U.S. Army—collection of the John F. Kennedy Library, Boston. p. 24, PFC Craig W. Hansell, 199th Inf. Bde., U.S. Army—collection of Peter Gyallay-Pap. p. 25, Sgt. John Gallo, U.S. Marine Corps. p. 26, George J. Denoncourt II, 1st Inf. Div., U.S., Army—collection of the John F. Kennedy Library, Boston. p. 27, top, Sgt. John Gallo, U.S. Marine Corps; bottom, Sp4 Brock, 221st Sig. Co., U.S. Army. p. 28, top, Sp4 Bob Hodierne, U.S. Army—*Pacific Stars & Stripes;* bottom, Sp4 James Lohr, 101st Abn. Div., U.S. Army. p. 29, JOC Robert Moeser, U.S. Navy. p. 30, PHC A. Hill, U.S. Navy. p. 31, top, CDR R.H. Sullivan, U.S. Navy; bottom, PHC L. Bernard Moran, U.S. Navy. p. 32, collection of Marv Wolf. p. 33, Sgt. Howard Breedlove, DASPO, U.S. Army. pp. 34, 35, 1LT Landon K. Thorne II, U.S. Marine Corps. pp. 36, 37, Sp5 William Stretch, 101st Abn. Div., U.S. Army. p. 38, 1LT Don Critchfield, 221st Sig. Co., U.S. Army. p. 39, Cpl. Brown, U.S. Marine Corps. p. 40, 1LT Don Critchfield, 221st Sig. Co., U.S. Army. p. 41, Sgt. John Gallo, U.S. Marine Corps. p. 42, Sp5 John Andescavage, 221st Sig. Co., U.S. Army. p. 43, Sgt. Marv Wolf, 1st Air Cavalry, U.S. Army. pp. 44-5, 46, Sgt. John Gallo, U.S. Marine Corps. p. 47, Sp4 Pearson, U.S. Army. p. 48, PFC Eugene Campbell, 523d Sig. Bn., U.S. Army. p. 49, Sp4 George J. Denoncourt II, 1st Inf. Div., U.S. Army—collection of the John F. Kennedy Library, Boston. p. 50, U.S. Army. p. 51, Sp4 Paul Halverson, U.S. Army. p. 52, Sgt. Bryan Grigsby, DASPO, U.S. Army; bottom, James McJunkin, 221st Sig. Co., U.S. Army. p. 53, Sp4 Alan Cahill, 221st Sig. Co., U.S. Army. p. 54, PFC E.E. Hildreth, U.S. Marine Corps. p. 55, Cpl. R.L. Pearson, U.S. Marine Corps. p. 56, top, Sgt. John Gallo, U.S. Marine Corps; bottom, 1LT Eric Wiegand, 221st Sig. Co., U.S. Army. p. 57, Sp4 James Pardue, U.S. Army. p. 58, top left, Sgt. G. Ross, 298th Sig. Co., U.S.

Army; top right, U.S. Army; bottom left, Sp5 Leonard Hekel, U.S. Army; bottom right, Sp4 Jerald Kringle, U.S. Army. p. 59, PFC J. Gonzales, 199th Inf. Bde., U.S. Army—collection of Peter Gyallay-Pap. p. 60, JOC Robert Moeser, U.S. Navy. p. 61, top, PFC Mincemoyer, U.S. Marine Corps; bottom, SSG K. Kelly, U.S. Marine Corps. p. 62, top, PFC Norman Weersing, U.S. Army; bottom, Sp4 Howard Nuernberger, 221st Sig. Co., U.S. Army. p. 63, Sgt. Doug Clifford, U.S. Air Force. p. 64, top, SSG Woltner, U.S. Marine Corps; bottom, U.S. Marine Corps. p. 65, Sp4 Howard Nuernberger, 221st Sig. Co., U.S. Army. p. 66, top, 1LT Landon K. Thorne II, U.S. Marine Corps. pp. 66, bottom, 67, 68, 69, Sgt. Marv Wolf, 1st Air Cavalry, U.S. Army. p. 70, top, 1LT Landon K. Thorne II, U.S. Marine Corps; bottom left, Sp4 Dwight Carter, 221st Sig. Co., U.S. Army; bottom right, PFC Stan Pratt, 593d Sig. Co., U.S. Army. p. 71, 1LT Nick Mills, 221st Sig. Co., U.S. Army. p. 72, top, 1LT David MacMillan, 221st Sig. Co., U.S. Army; bottom left, Bill Hackwell, U.S. Air Force; bottom right, PFC Stan Pratt, 593d Sig. Co., U.S. Army. p. 73, collection of Doug Clifford. p. 74, top, Sgt. John Gallo, U.S. Marine Corps; bottom, Sp4 Peter Gyallay-Pap, 199th Inf. Bde., U.S. Army. p. 75, Sp4 Dwight Carter, 221st Sig. Co., U.S. Army. p. 76, top, Sp4 Bob Hodierne, U.S. Army—*Pacific Stars & Stripes;* bottom, Sp4 George J. Denoncourt II, 1st Inf. Div., U.S. Army—collection of the John F. Kennedy Library, Boston. p. 77, Sp4 John Olson, U.S. Army. p. 78, Sgt. Doug Clifford, U.S. Air Force. p. 79, Dick Durrance, DASPO, U.S. Army. p. 80, Sp4 John Olson, U.S. Army. p. 81, Sp4 Bruce Montoya, 13th Sig. Bn., U.S. Army. p. 82, Sp4 George J. Denoncourt II, 1st Inf. Div., U.S. Army—collection of the John F. Kennedy Library, Boston. p. 83, top, PHC L. Bernard Moran, U.S. Navy; bottom, JO1 W.B. Bass, Jr., U.S. Navy. p. 84, U.S. Army. p. 85, Sgt. Al Wiegand, U.S. Marine Corps. p. 86, top, Cpl. B.L. Axelrod, U.S. Marine Corps; bottom, Sp4 Craig W. Hansell, 199th Inf. Bde., U.S. Army—collection of Peter Gyallay-Pap. p. 87, top, PFC David Epstein, 69th Sig. Bn., U.S. Army; bottom, Sp4 Dwight Carter, 221st Sig. Co., U.S. Army. pp. 88-9, SSG Shearer, U.S. Marine Corps. pp. 90-5, Sp4 Bob Hodierne, U.S. Army—*Pacific Stars & Stripes.* pp. 96, 97, PH1 Dan Dodd, U.S. Navy. p. 98, top, PH2 C.B. Hall, U.S. Navy; bottom, PH1 R.H. Elder, U.S. Navy. pp. 99-105, Chip Maury, SEAL Team One, U.S. Navy. pp. 106, 107, Sp4 James Lohr, 101st Abn. Div., U.S. Army. p. 108, top, PFC Cole, U.S. Marine Corps; bottom, U.S. Army. p. 109, top, Sp5 William Cunningham, 9th Inf. Div., U.S. Army; bottom, U.S. Army. p. 110, top, Sgt. Berni Mangiboyant, U.S. Army; bottom, Sp5 John Andescavage, 221st Sig. Co., U.S. Army. p. 111, collection of Frank Lee. pp. 112-15, Sp4 Bob Hodierne, U.S. Army—*Pacific Stars & Stripes.* p. 116, LCpl. C.W. Wright, U.S. Marine Corps. p. 117, collection of Doug Woods. p. 118, Cpl. Doug Woods, U.S. Marine Corps. p. 119, top, U.S. Marine Corps; bottom, JOC Robert Moeser, U.S. Navy. p. 120, Sgt. R.R. Neuber, U.S. Marine Corps. p. 121, U.S. Army. p. 122, 1LT Don Critchfield, 221st Sig. Co., U.S. Army. pp. 123-5, Sp4 John Olson, U.S. Army. p. 126, Sp5 Ed Scott, 221st Sig. Co., U.S. Army—collection of Nick Mills. p. 127, top, Sp4 Howard Nuernberger, 221st Sig. Co., U.S. Army; bottom, 1LT Nick Mills, 221st Sig. Co., U.S. Army. p. 128, Sp4 Peter Gyallay-Pap, 199th Inf. Bde., U.S. Army. p. 129, top, U.S. Marine Corps; bottom, Sp4 Frank Mitchell, 221st Sig. Co., U.S. Army. p. 130, 1LT Chuck Cook, SEAPC, U.S. Army. p. 131, Chris Bunge, U.S. Air Force. pp. 132-6, Sp4 Ronald Haeberle, 11th Inf. Bde., Americal Div., U.S. Army—LIFE Magazine, © 1968, Time Inc. p. 138, top, U.S. Army; bottom, Sgt. Bryan Grigsby, DASPO, U.S. Army. p. 139, U.S. Army. p. 140, top, Sgt. Bryan Grigsby, DASPO, U.S. Army; bottom, PFC David Epstein, 69th Sig. Bn., U.S. Army. p. 141, Sgt. John Gallo, U.S. Marine Corps. p. 142, top, Sp4 Pearson, 53d Sig. Bn., U.S. Army; bottom, Sp4 John Olson, U.S. Army. p. 143, top, collection of Joseph Tourtelot; bottom, U.S. Army (NVA photo). p. 144, top, SSG Alfred Batungbacal, DASPO, U.S. Army; bottom, Sp5 Darrell DuRall, 39th Sig. Bn., U.S. Army. p. 145, Sgt. Howard Breedlove, DASPO, U.S. Army. p. 146, top, Sp4 Mike Laley, 69th Sig. Bn., U.S. Army; bottom, Sp5 John Gardenhire, U.S. Army. p. 147, U.S. Army—collection of William Kelly. p. 148, Sp5 Glenn Rasmussen, 69th Sig. Bn., U.S. Army. p. 149, U.S. Army. pp. 150-1, 152, Sp4 L. Cundiff, 221st Sig. Co., U.S. Army. p. 153, Sp5 Randall Reimer, 53d Sig. Bn., U.S. Army. p. 154, C.A. Hinton, U.S. Navy. p. 155, top, Sp5 Randall Reimer, 53d Sig. Bn., U.S. Army; bottom, Sgt. F.E. Burch, U.S. Marine

Corps. p. 156, 1LT Don Critchfield, 221st Sig. Co., U.S. Army. p. 157, Bill Hackwell, U.S. Air Force. p. 158, DASPO, U.S. Army—collection of Leroy Massie. p. 159, top, Sp4 James Lohr, 101st Abn. Div., U.S. Army; bottom, Bill Hackwell, U.S. Air Force. p. 160, PH3 J.L. Agwegan, U.S. Navy. p. 161, top, U.S. Marine Corps; bottom, PH3 Harold Brown, U.S. Navy. p. 162, K.R. Eason, U.S. Marine Corps. p. 163, Sgt. Bryan Grigsby, DASPO, U.S. Army. p. 164, Chip Maury, SEAL Team One, U.S. Navy. p. 166, M/Sgt. Al Chang, U.S. Army. p. 167, Sp4 John Olson, U.S. Army. p. 168, top, U.S. Navy; bottom, Sgt. Marv Wolf, 1st Air Cavalry, U.S. Army. p. 169, top, YN2 H.E. Stramler, U.S. Navy; bottom, Sp4 Howard Nuernberger, 221st Sig. Co., U.S. Army. p. 170, left, Sp4 Bob Hodierne, U.S. Army—*Pacific Stars & Stripes;* top & bottom right, Dick Durrance, DASPO, U.S. Army. p. 171, M/Sgt. Al Chang, U.S. Army. p. 172, U.S. Marine Corps. p. 173, Sp5 Jerry Wyngarden, 199th Inf. Bde., U.S. Army—collection of Peter Gyallay-Pap. p. 174, Dick Durrance, DASPO, U.S. Army. p. 175, Sgt. John Gallo, U.S. Marine Corps.

The article on page 92 appears courtesy of *Pacific Stars & Stripes.*

Books, Reports, & Periodicals:
Hersh, Seymour. *My Lai 4.* Random, 1970.

Lewinski, Jorge. *The Camera at War.* Simon & Schuster, 1978.

McJunkin, James N., and Max D. Crace. *Visions of Vietnam.* Presidio Press, 1983.

Peers, Lt. Gen. W.R. *The My Lai Inquiry.* Norton, 1979.

The *New York Times,* the *Army Times, Pacific Stars & Stripes,* the *Vietnam War Newsletter, Leatherneck Magazine, Soldier of Fortune* Magazine.

Institutions & Organizations:
The Defense Audio-Visual Agency, Washington, D.C.

The John F. Kennedy Library, Boston, Mass.
Department of the Navy, Office of Information, Washington, D.C.
The Vietnam Veterans Arts Group

The Vietnam Veterans Outreach Program

The Marine Corps Combat Correspondents Association

Acknowledgments
The author and editors wish to thank the following individuals for their generous assistance:

Claude Bache, Tom Bartlett, Charles Beresford, Geoff Boehm, Robert Carlisle, Carl Conn, Heather C. Conover, Chuck Cook, Judy Cook, George Esper, Frank Faulkner, Ray Goddard, Ronald Haeberle, Tom Hebert, Clay Hollister, Haney Howell, John Keller, Gary Krull, Logan McMinn, David Miller, Paul Moulton, Michael Murphy, Michelle O'Brien, Martin Pilsch, Bob Poos, Gerald Pulley, Peter Ruplenas, Jack Seifert, John Shimashita, James Straub, and Paul Thomas.